THE FISH EYES TRILOGY

the *Fish Eyes* *Trilogy*

Fish Eyes
Boys With Cars
Let Me Borrow That Top

by ANITA MAJUMDAR
illustrated by
MARIA NGUYEN

BANFF CENTRE PRESS
Banff

PLAYWRIGHTS CANADA PRESS
Toronto

For professional or amateur production rights, please contact:
The Playwrights Guild of Canada
401 Richmond Street West, Suite 350
Toronto, ON M5V 3A8
416-703-0201, orders@playwrightsguild.ca

LIBRARY AND ARCHIVES CANADA CATALOGUING IN PUBLICATION
Majumdar, Anita, author
       The fish eyes trilogy / Anita Majumdar ; with illustrations by Maria
Nguyen.

Plays.
Co-published by: Banff Centre Press.
Contents: Fish eyes -- Boys with cars -- Let me borrow that top
Issued in print and electronic formats.
ISBN 978-1-77091-327-1 (paperback).--ISBN 978-1-77091-328-8 (pdf).--
ISBN 978-1-77091-329-5 (html).--ISBN 978-1-77091-546-6 (mobi)

       I. Nguyen, Maria, illustrator II. Title.

PS8626.A421F58 2015   C812'.6   C2015-906910-6
                                                  C2015-906911-4

We acknowledge the financial support of the Canada Council for the Arts, the Ontario Arts Council (OAC), the Ontario Media Development Corporation, and the Government of Canada through the Canada Book Fund for our publishing activities. Nous remercions l'appui financier du Conseil des Arts du Canada, le Conseil des arts de l'Ontario (CAO), la Société de développement de l'industrie des médias de l'Ontario, et le Gouvernement du Canada par l'entremise du Fonds du livre du Canada pour nos activités d'édition.

Canada Council
for the Arts

Conseil des arts
du Canada

ONTARIO ARTS COUNCIL
CONSEIL DES ARTS DE L'ONTARIO
an Ontario government agency
un organisme du gouvernement de l'Ontario

Canada

Ontario
Ontario Media Development
Corporation

For Gregory Prest.
It started with us.

As Canada's leading arts and cultural institution, The Banff Centre has a long history of providing artists of all disciplines—including actors, writers, and performing arts practitioners—at every stage of their careers, with the tools, techniques, and time to test their creative ideas. This is how we began as the Banff School of Drama in 1933.

At a time when local theatre groups were beginning to flourish nationwide, the failing economy put a stop to touring shows and the development of theatre artists, audiences, and, for many, their communities. Identifying a need, the University of Alberta's Department of Extension responded by offering a single course in drama in the stunning Rocky Mountains in Banff, Alberta. A few years later, courses in creative writing and playwriting were added to the repertoire, and the school was renamed The Banff School of Fine Arts. Today, The Banff Centre stands as a globally recognized leader in the development and dissemination of contemporary arts, with multidisciplinary programming in opera, dance, visual and digital arts, literary arts, music, Indigenous arts, film and media arts, and more.

Although our campus has grown from an old auditorium on Banff Avenue to forty-four acres on the side of Sleeping Buffalo Mountain, our commitment to creating opportunities for artists to learn from the very best talent in the world, to develop themselves and new work, has stayed the same. Our creative residencies give artists the opportunity to develop, build, rehearse, and perform original material in one of the most inspiring places in the world, leading to the commissioning of over fifty new works and the debut of over one hundred and fifty more every year. From multidisciplinary theatre and dance projects to visual and digital arts installations and exhibitions, music performances in conventional and unconventional spaces, and new voices in storytelling in the literary and digital narrative worlds, we're proud to champion new artistic voices.

When John Murrell chose to mentor Canadian actress, playwright, and dancer Anita Majumdar as part of the Governor General's Performing Arts Awards Mentorship Program in 2013, we were delighted to offer them both a two-week self-directed residency in our Leighton Artists' Colony. Nestled in a wooded area on The Banff Centre campus, the Colony gives artists in all genres the time and space to create in a retreat environment, free from daily pressures and distractions.

Anita returned in 2014 and 2015 as a participant in the Playwrights Colony, one of our flagship residencies dedicated to giving Canadian playwrights a stimulating and collaborative space in which to work on their plays. With the support of director Brian Quirt, as well as actors at her disposal to assist with reading and workshopping scenes, Anita readied *The Fish Eyes Trilogy* for presentation in the Margaret Greenham Theatre. The show continues to tour extensively across Canada and around the world, and has been nominated for a Dora Mavor Moore Award. It's a joy to be able to share this with you now.

In this audacious trilogy of plays—*Fish Eyes*, *Boys With Cars*, and *Let Me Borrow That Top*—Anita shares the coming-of-age stories of three teenage girls who attend the same high school and process their real-life dramas through dance, while tackling issues related to feminism, cultural appropriation, and colonialism. Though rooted in South Asian culture, each story invites us to consider the joy and awkwardness of youth that resonates with all Canadians, regardless of our heritage. We empathize with Meena's struggle to be a *normal* high-school girl. And we feel Naz's heartache when her university plans begin to crumble. A classically trained Indian dancer herself, Anita worked closely with Maria Nguyen to include a series of illustrations in the text that give insight into the author's thinking and highlight the dance that is central to the stage production.

The Fish Eyes Trilogy is also the fourth Banff Centre co-publication with Playwrights Canada Press. The first was a trio of plays that included *Arigato, Tokyo* by Daniel MacIvor, *Armstrong's War* by Colleen Murphy, and *This is War* by Hannah Moscovitch, the first piece of dramatic literature to receive the Trillium Book Award in 2013.

We are proud of our partnership with Playwrights Canada Press, which shares with us a commitment to nurturing new and important contributions to the Canadian arts landscape. We look forward to many more exciting collaborations!

—Carolyn Warren
Vice President, Arts
The Banff Centre

The pleasures of working on *The Fish Eyes Trilogy* with Anita constitute a journey of more than four years since she first shared material with me and Producer Rupal Shah at the Nightswimming office in 2011. At the centre of that journey has been the beauty of watching a conversation between plot, character, dance, setting, music, image, performance, and performer evolve across three complex, interlocking stories. In the process, the trilogy has become a single, epic play anchored by a remarkable performance from Anita herself. Anita's journey with the plays has been much longer, stretching back to the creation of its first part, *Fish Eyes*, more than a decade ago, and stretching ahead to future productions of the plays, including an adaptation of parts two and three for teen audiences currently in development.

The story of this story begins with Anita creating and performing *Fish Eyes* while attending the National Theatre School in the early 2000s, then collaborating with her classmate Gregory Prest as director to create a full-length solo piece with runs in Toronto, Vancouver, India, and more. That play and its charismatic performance introduced many of us to Anita and contributed to a vital and important blossoming of South Asian Canadian theatre artists. *Fish Eyes* is Anita at her best—comic, political, inseparable from dance—embedded in the experience of a teen named Meena who is, like so many teens, deeply aware of her condition and deeply unaware of how she fits into the larger picture of her world. That contradiction makes for great comedy and a moving story; it also inspired Anita to want to return to the high-school world of the story as an experienced playwright and explore deeply a character who is far more aware of how the world is holding her back.

In early 2012, during her tenure as our playwright-in-residence, Anita read us a first draft of *Boys With Cars*, bringing to life Naz, another teenager struggling with the straitjacket of high school in Port Moody, BC. That reading was, I recall, a tough one as Anita herself struggled to find the heart of Naz's battle, but it was also a critical moment in the trilogy's development as it began to reveal that the school assembly that appears in *Fish Eyes* would become the central event of each of the three plays. That assembly binds Meena, Naz, and Candice in ways that none of them fully realize but ultimately offers the audience a challenging, painful, cathartic, and unexpected window into women negotiating a pathway into adulthood. We loved Naz's voice, and the new voice that Anita herself was discovering as a playwright. Nightswimming commissioned the play and committed to developing it with her.

Public presentations of *Boys With Cars* were essential to its development since dance sequences are integrated into the storytelling. Dance is so important that this volume features illustrations by Maria Nguyen capturing key choreographic images that Anita uses to tell her overlapping stories. These are plays of words; the teenagers are wordsmiths and demand to be heard even as no one seems to listen. But each also speaks with her body, when she dances of course, but also when each tries to command the spaces from which their high school and its denizens want to constrain her.

As the new play evolved, the school gym that appears twice in *Fish Eyes* reappeared as a battleground in the final scene of *Boys*. And as it did, a third play began to take shape for Anita, unexpectedly tackling the hidden truths of Candice, nemesis of Meena and Naz, who has her own villains to fight. Once again, we commissioned Anita and she dove into language, also finding a new vocabulary of image and physicality in the form of the YouTube makeup tutorial. As *Let Me Borrow That Top* took shape, our dramaturgical adventure was to align the chronology and events and locations of three stories, pushing us backward to a revision of *Fish Eyes*, deeper into *Boys*, and then forward to further refinements of *Top* that made Candice's story inevitable but no less tragic.

With the three individual stories now alive, we produced a work-in-progress showcase of the full trilogy in late 2013, complete with an Indian meal during intermission. Several presenters attended and following a residency at the 2014 Banff Centre Playwrights Colony to further refine the storytelling across the full trilogy, a premiere national tour came together, with The Banff Centre offering added support as the co-commissioner of *Let Me Borrow That Top*.

The dramaturgical process has been a delicate dance between text and movement, from conversations between playwright, dramaturg/director, and producer about what happens to which woman in which play, to studio sessions in which Anita found the physical life of each teen and choreographed dances unique to each. Touring was also critical to the evolution of the trilogy, as contributions of all members of the creative team to the production and the audiences to whom we told these stories inspired Anita to further refinements of the text.

The tour included a double bill of part one and two at the Great Canadian Theatre Company in which *Boys With Cars* premiered, and then the premiere of the full trilogy, performed in rep, at the PuSh International Performing Arts Festival. That run at the Cultch culminated beautifully with all three parts performed in a single day with a meal break between part one and two.

Throughout these many workshops, readings, residencies, and rehearsals, the vision driving us forward was the idea of presenting the three parts as a single performance with two intermissions, a dream ultimately realized at Victoria's Belfry Theatre on March 15, 2015. This glorious event affirmed all of Anita's instincts about the layers of her storytelling, the power of the body to convey emotional complexity, and the magic that a solo performer can weave. *The Fish Eyes Trilogy* insists that we listen with our eyes, hear with our hearts, and see the other in each of us.

—Brian Quirt
Artistic Director
Nightswimming

Anita Majumdar's work exposes uncomfortable truths about how it feels to be perceived as "other." Stories about South Asian Canadian women are rare, not only in the Canadian theatre landscape but on screen and in the media. When we are included, the many nuances of our varied Canadian experiences are often reduced into a narrative about honour killings, about stereotypical domineering parents who are unwilling to bend to the "freer values of the West." In *The Fish Eyes Trilogy*, Anita provides an antidote to our absence and over-simplification by writing intelligent, imperfect, and unforgettable South Asian Canadian female characters.

In *Fish Eyes*, Meena's desperate desire to shed her "otherness" while simultaneously depending on her South Asian cultural identity to help create her sense of self is a common Canadian paradox. Kalyani Aunty is a living relic in a new land, holding on to what she knows, passing knowledge down in the hopes that her students' successes will justify the choices she has made. Through Meena and Kalyani Aunty, we experience a parent-child dynamic that mirrors the experiences of immigrant families across Canada.

In *Boys With Cars*, Naz's overwhelming feeling of unease and discomfort with her small hometown comes from the growing realization that as a young woman of colour, the world is not on her side. During the school assembly that links all three plays, Naz wishes she could trade places with the privileged Candice. Her desire to do so stems largely from her immediate trauma, but also partly from a clearer, bitter understanding that the rules are different for her than they are for Candice.

Candice is, in many ways, a complicating factor. For the first two parts of the trilogy she exemplifies the pretty, skinny, villainous blonde. As audience members, we may not always like Meena and Naz, but we are on their sides and Candice becomes our enemy too. The fact that we learn in *Let Me Borrow That Top* that Candice has significant challenges of her own doesn't devalue our feelings about her, it complicates them. We are reminded that it is rarely ever a privilege to be a girl, regardless of race. Candice is one of the many desirable fish from Kalyani Aunty's parable at the end of *Fish Eyes*—perfect and edible, never thrown back, and always consumed.

The Fish Eyes Trilogy is funny, uncomfortable, and demanding. It demands that we recognize the particular challenges that young women face in a society that has failed them in so many ways. It demands that we see South Asian women as individuals, not symbols. By writing these plays, Anita is demanding that we accept the validity, the legitimacy, and the heterogeneity of the "South Asian Canadian Experience."

—Rupal Shah
Producer
Nightswimming

The Fish Eyes Trilogy was commissioned, developed, and produced by Nightswimming with development support from The Banff Centre. *Boys With Cars* was commissioned and developed by Nightswimming; *Let Me Borrow That Top* was co-commissioned by Nightswimming and The Banff Centre, and developed by Nightswimming.

The national tour of *The Fish Eyes Trilogy* included the Great Canadian Theatre Company (Ottawa), the PuSh International Performing Arts Festival (Vancouver), the Aga Khan Museum (Toronto), the Belfry Theatre (Victoria), and The Banff Centre.

The playwright is extremely grateful to The Banff Centre for their generous support and for the assistance of the 2014 Banff Playwrights Colony—a partnership between The Banff Centre and the Canada Council for the Arts.

The Fish Eyes Trilogy premiered at the Cultch, Vancouver, on January 31, 2015, with the following cast and creative team:

Choreographer and actor: Anita Majumdar
Director and dramaturg: Brian Quirt
Producer: Rupal Shah
Stage manager: Sandy Plunkett
Lighting design: Rebecca Picherack
Set and costume design: Jackie Chau
Projection and sound design: Christopher Stanton
Production manager: Simon Rossiter

FISH EYES

Fish Eyes premiered at Theatre Passe Muraille, Toronto, in October 2005 as part of the Stage 3 Repertory Theatre Series with the following cast and creative team:

Choreographer and actor: Anita Majumdar
Director and dramaturg: Gregory David Prest
Stage manager: Marie Fewer-Muncic
Set and lighting design: Steve Lucas

Fish Eyes was first presented at the André Pagé Studio at the National Theatre School of Canada in January 2004, directed and dramaturged by Kate Schlemmer, and performed and choreographed by Anita Majumdar. The play went on to be presented at the SummerWorks Theatre Festival in August 2004 with Gregory David Prest as director and dramaturg, which was followed by a workshop performance as part of Harbourfront Theatre's Hatch Program with Marie Fewer-Muncic acting as stage manager and lighting designer. *Fish Eyes* went on to be performed in multiple locations after its premiere at Theatre Passe Muraille, including the Museum Theatre in Chennai, India, in 2006; the Gateway Theatre in Richmond, BC, in 2007; the Belfry Theatre in 2012; and the Agha Khan Museum in 2015. The play was further developed with Nightswimming Theatre as part of *The Fish Eyes Trilogy* commission in 2013.

Characters

Meena
Kalyani Aunty
Buddy
Candice

KALYANI AUNTY is sitting on her stool with a tray of flowers in her lap and her ankles adorned in dancer bells. She performs a bharatanatyam hand-gesture series, silently narrating the Fisherperson Story. She ends with the gesture for "one with eyes like a fish." KALYANI AUNTY lifts the tray from her lap, performs a short prayer towards the Natraj statue behind her, and then turns to the audience.

KALYANI AUNTY: Namaste and welcome! Okay, okay, I know you be asking, where is dance, WHERE IS "Nimbooda"?! "Nimbooda" is here only! Oh. Okay. You white people must be asking, "What is this 'Nimbooda'?" "Nimbooda" is lemon and lime, two in one! See, good Indian girl be asking for nice, juicy, tangy, lemon-lime "Nimbooda"! But lemon-lime is code . . . for lover! <*tsk*> Mmm, tasty, no?

Brothers and sisters, please let me present my darling student, Meenakshi Kumari, dancing "Nimbooda"!

Stomp.

KALYANI AUNTY turns away. MEENA turns out, sees the audience, and stares at them. With a disgruntled sigh, she signals to the stage manager to start the music with a thumbs-up. MEENA's face becomes bright and smiling as she executes a dance full of energy married to an old-world precision and grace. A beat after landing in her final triumphant dance pose, MEENA eyes the audience and tries to maintain her positive attitude, but stumbles as she explains her performance.

MEENA: Hi. My name's Meena. It's short for Meenakshi. It means fish eyes. Dancing since I was five. Yeah, it's a real gift. And that little number you saw me doing? That's the Lemon-Lime Lover Dance . . . "Nimbooda"? Yeah, I don't really get it either. Sorry, I guess I should be more excited.

Stomp. Stomp.

She dances a hand gesture across her face that changes her expression to a superficial "dance happy."

I love being an Indian dancer! And the questions about "the dot" NEVER get old! I

LOVE how Indian dance gets into everything I do! For example, brushing my teeth!

MEENA *pulls out a toothbrush and dances a short but impressive classical Indian phrase in front of the bathroom mirror. She ends by spitting out the toothpaste into the bathroom sink in front of her.*

It's a great quality to have when you're seventeen!

She breaks out of her "dance happy" expression.

Yeah, I'm so happy that for every weekend of my life my parents dragged me out to some random basement owned by Kalyani Aunty . . . Her name means "happy cow" in case you wondered. She thinks the British are planning a second invasion, so she stockpiles her closets full of emergency curry powder, coconut milk, and toilet paper.

She's not even really my aunt, either; we call anyone who's Indian and old aunty or uncle to make it seem like we're all a big, happy family. Well, the amount of time I spend at Kalyani Aunty's house, I might as well be a part of the family!

Stomp. Stomp.

MEENA dances a short phrase to emphasize her point.

Flashback: KALYANI AUNTY appears before us in her basement dance studio with her class of students, who are all trying to avoid looking her in the eye.

KALYANI AUNTY: LALITA, NO! This is not acceptable. Looking so Humpty Dumpty! How can I let you keep dancing? Tell me? No, tell me! I open to suggestion! Audience? They not nice like Aunty.

They laugh at such fatty-fatty girl on stage. No. Nothing doing. Chips, hamburger, pizza . . . FINISH. Indian girl, Indian dancer eat Indian food!

Stomp.

Return to the present.

MEENA: I mean, Jesus Christ! Who says that? And if that isn't the obese happy-cow-pot calling the kettle black. But now it's senior year and everyone's living the dream! All the normal girls are going to Andrew Dubielek's parties—you know, DUBEE—and going to Golden Spike Fest in the summer; and making out in bushes with hot, popular boys like Buddy Cain; and drinking lots of beer! And making best friends with popular girls like Candice Paskis because she holds your hair back while you throw up! But where am I? I'm performing at, like, the summer Lord Ganesh Festival. All those weekend trips to Vancouver, driving around with Kalyani Aunty, drinking Thums Up. Oh. Thums Up is India's national brand of cola. It kinda tastes like Pepsi. If you're good at using your imagination!

At least I wasn't the only dancer. Like me and Lalita, and Sukhi and Pavan, we all shared the same hell. Sometimes we went out to see Bollywood movies after dance class . . . Not that I watch a lot of Bollywood movies. Not like other people. I mean, I'm pretty busy; it's my grad year, right?

MEENA quickly grabs her school backpack and digs out her Bollywood scrapbook.

But me and Lalita and Sukhi and Pavan are for sure going to see the Aishwarya Rai Movie Retrospective!

She holds the scrapbook above her head to show off a clipped-out picture of the retrospective poster.

Which aren't Bollywood movies because they're playing in the white-people theatres. But THE Aishwarya Rai Movie Retrospective has my favourite actress—Aishwarya Rai . . . you know? Nineteen Ninety-Four Miss World Turned Bollywood Superstar AISHWARYA RAI? She's *so* pretty, and she has these grey-coloured eyes, and she studied classical Indian dance when she was little just like me. And some people even think we kinda look alike?

She puts her head close to the picture for the audience to examine the similarities for themselves.

Well, I'm not as tall, but there's a resemblance. Anyway, I know all her movie songs . . . HIT IT!

MEENA nods to the stage manager and "Nimbooda" plays. MEENA recognizes the song right away.

Oh, that's like an insult to my intelligence! That's obviously just the Lemon-Lime Lover Dance, "Nimbooda"! I heard she danced so hard she bled from her feet! HIT IT!

MEENA nods to the stage manager again and "Ishq Kameena" plays. MEENA recognizes the song.

OH! That's from . . . *Shakti*! But it's kind of a trick because she only had a guest appearance in the movie? HIT IT!

MEENA nods to the stage manager again and a remixed version of "Ramta Jogi" plays. MEENA takes some time to recognize the song, but once she does she grooves to the music.

That's such a trick! It's SUCH a trick because it's a remix of the original song, but it's from *Taal*! I know because she was only in three movies that year, but she still managed to get the Filmfare Best Actress Award!

The music stops. Beat. MEENA looks at the picture of Aishwarya Rai in her scrapbook.

Nineteen Ninety-Four Miss World Turned Bollywood Superstar AISHWARYA RAI makes me feel so proud because when people talk about how much they like her, it's kinda like they're talking about how much they like me. And when Julia Roberts calls her the most beautiful woman in the world, it's like Julia Roberts is calling ME the most beautiful woman in the world!

MEENA puts away her backpack and performs a classical Indian dance phrase. Flashback: KALYANI AUNTY appears in her basement dance studio.

Stomp.

KALYANI AUNTY: You know, girls, when I come to this country I no speak no damn English, but now speaking first-class English. Aunty tell you secret? Aunty watch TV, watch *Three's Company*! What do you mean you don't KNOW *Three's Company*? Where the hell you've been living, man?!

She dances while singing the first two lines of the Three's Company theme song.

. . . And John Ritter? Comic genius! And so good looking! Too bad he died.

KALYANI AUNTY'S cellphone rings.

Girls! You hear that? Phone ringing! *Chalo*! Practise footwork . . . now, NOW!

MEENA begrudgingly begins doing footwork exercises on the spot. KALYANI AUNTY answers her phone.

Hallo? HALLO?! Talk to me! Oh, Gurumaa-*ji*? What a pleasant surprise!

MEENA continues her footwork as she speaks.

MEENA: That's the Sunday morning phone call from Gurumaa-*ji*, Kalyani Aunty's dance teacher from when she was little. Kalyani Aunty makes us practise footwork by the phone to show Gurumaa-*ji* we're working extra hard. But it's like a forty-five-minute waste of money, 'cause they never talk about anything!

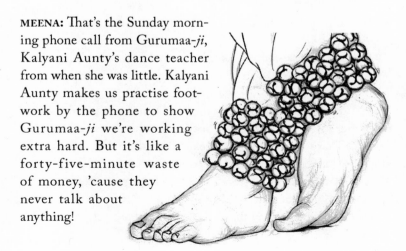

KALYANI AUNTY: *(into her phone) Haan,* Gurumaa-*ji*? No, I very angry at you. I call you, you no call me back? Heh? *Indian Idol*? TELL ME EVERYTHING!

MEENA is still doing her footwork.

MEENA: Whenever Kalyani Aunty was on the phone talking with Gurumaa-*ji*, I sort of *went away.*

MEENA's footwork moves her into a fantasy dreamscape.

Like I'd start thinking about stuff . . . like Buddy? Buddy Cain?! He's like my John Ritter . . . Oh, only he's alive! Oh yeah, he's totally alive! At first, I didn't start out liking Buddy so much. I just thought he was really handsome and had a nice face! And that was way back in grade seven, so you can only imagine how love grows when it festers in the heart. I just made that up right now! I have these love stories I made up about me and Buddy. But you have to be careful of that sort of thing because it's sort of like having a relationship with yourself!

MEENA abruptly stops her footwork when she realizes what she's just revealed. She buries her face in her hands.

This is so embarrassing! I really want to be normal, and I'm gonna be! Grad 2013. The last dance of the year! I know this is my big chance! That's why I'm gonna wear this tight red dress . . . with SHOES! And I'm gonna look just as pretty as Nineteen Ninety-Four Miss World Turned Bollywood Superstar AISHWARYA RAI from her summer of '99 blockbuster hit movie *Hum Dil De Chuke Sanam*! Everyone's gonna notice. Buddy Cain's gonna notice.

*A sunny Rajasthani desert appears and the song "Man Mohini"
underscores the scene, replicating the opening of the Aishwarya
Rai film* Hum Dil De Chuke Sanam. MEENA *dances through
the desert using Aishwarya Rai dance movements from the film.*

I'm just gonna walk in and toss my hair like Aishwarya does in
the big desert opening scene, and there's this fan blowing from
somewhere. And from across the sandy room—Grad's gonna have
an Arabian desert theme! And Buddy's wearing these flashy gold
harem chaps and he has this lasso and he sees me and he realizes
he's in love with me, even though we come from such different,
different worlds.

MEENA acts out the following as Indian-danced role-play.

At first I act like I don't even notice him, but that just gets him more passionate and he grabs me, but I push him away, so then he has to prove himself to me through song and dance!

A Bollywood version of "Pretty Woman" plays. Suddenly we are transported to a high-school graduation dance and BUDDY appears dancing to "Pretty Woman" like a Bollywood hero. The offstage stage manager stops the music abruptly. BUDDY, along with the fantasy, disappear. MEENA is caught alone on stage. Looking around, she discovers and picks up a beach ball.

And then me and Buddy hang out all summer and realize how we're totally meant to be. I mean, I don't know exactly *what* we're going to do, but we probably hold hands, and walk down the beach, and then he chases me down the beach and spins me around by my waist and then we fall in the water—and we laugh, but I pretend to be mad. And then we splash water at each other and he tries to dunk me but we kiss instead!

MEENA finds herself lying on top of BUDDY. She slowly French kisses him. The Bollywood version of "Pretty Woman" plays again and MEENA finds herself lying on top of the beach ball and not BUDDY, but she doesn't care and pushes the ball aside to Bollywood dance to "Pretty Woman" on the beach as though her life depended on it. After the song ends, KALYANI AUNTY's footwork bleeds into MEENA's fantasy and transitions us back to the basement dance studio.

KALYANI AUNTY: *(on her phone)* Gurumaa-*ji*? *Haan*, we practising very hard for All India Dance Competition 2013. *Haan*, I working Meena extra hard, doing EXTREME "Nimbooda" . . . I say, EXTREME "Nimbooda" . . . *Haan* . . . Oh, we make you proud, Gurumaa-*ji*! I really feeling like this going to be summer of *Meena and Kalyani Aunty*! . . . <tsk> . . . I say, SUMMER OF MEENA and KALYANI AUNTY! *Uff*! Digga-digga DHA, digga-digga DHA, digga-digga dha-DHA!

KALYANI AUNTY hangs up the phone and exits. MEENA appears in isolation.

MEENA: I'm sorry. "The Summer of Meena and Kalyani Aunty"? What about "The Summer of Meena and Buddy"?! I'm practically a grown woman; I'm going to be graduated from high school soon! And who knows, if I play my cards right I might even be married after Grad 2013! But none of that's gonna happen if I'm over in India dancing in a stupid dance competition. I need to secure my position as Buddy's girlfriend-slash-life partner. I just need to tell Kalyani Aunty that I'm not going to India and that she should just find somebody else! Yeah!

MEENA goes to find KALYANI AUNTY but runs into the Natraj statue instead. They meet eyes. MEENA assumes the Natraj statue's pose and turns back to her audience.

Um . . . I think I'll just do that later.

MEENA points to the stage manager.

HIT IT!

A remixed version of "Dola Re Dola" (from the Aishwarya Rai film, Devdas*) plays. MEENA is transported to the set of* Devdas *and dances in the centre like Aishwarya Rai. She loses herself in the movement in the centre of the dance floor. KALYANI AUNTY arrives and watches MEENA till the end of the dance and then gestures for MEENA to come over to her. Flashback: A post–dance recital house party.*

KALYANI AUNTY: MEENA! Come here, talk to Aunty! We have friendly chat.

So you have boyfriend? Well, you no want to end up alone. You remember Balakrishna Jeetendra Mahendra Dharmendra Kishwar Pyarelal Prakash Das Gupta? *Hai* Krishna! What a catch, Balakrishna Jeetendra Mahendra Dharmendra Kishwar Pyarelal Prakash Das Gupta. Okay, okay, okay, OKAY! So, Balakrishna Jeetendra Mahendra . . . let's just call him BJ, okay? So. BJ not so good-looking. Not so much of hair. Little dark, fat, no have car . . . But BJ SMART! How many forty-year-old you know be having own dairy farm. AND? M.B.A. from Fansi Utaar Fanaa University, you know, FU-FU? BJ bride live like dairy QUEEN!

MEENA: Yeah, I don't know; I kinda wanna be with someone who's cool and has a nice face. Like someone who does athletic things like football and track and field and has to take his shirt off lots!

But someone who's really nice to people . . . Like . . . LIKE . . . a real superhero!

KALYANI AUNTY: Well, you know what being really super? Really "cool"? Being chartered accountant! YEAH! Have big-big power . . . power to calculate! Analyze data . . . Crunching number? WITH HIS BRAIN! Ahhhh! Aunty can't breathe! BJ too cool! Oh Meena. You take BJ? Be happy woman!

Shift to gym class. MEENA *gets a water bottle and starts doing jumping jacks in the middle of the gym.*

MEENA: I hate this—I hate this—I hate this—I hate this—I hate this—I hate this—I hate this—I hate this—I hate this—I hate this!

She takes a drink from her water bottle.

So this is the hell I have to put up with THREE times a week! And this is just the warm-up! NO WATER—YES, MISS FLEMMING!!

She runs on the spot.

You think they would've gotten rid of gym class along with the canings! But we have to pointlessly run around in circles for twenty minutes so we can prepare for physical challenges like dodge ball and badminton! But I kind of like how the wind goes through my hair because it's like—

We are transported to the Hum Dil De Chuke Sanam *fantasy desert again. The "Man Mohini" song underscores.*

—Nineteen Ninety-Four Miss World Turned Bollywood Superstar AISHWARYA RAI running through the desert in *Hum Dil De Chuke Sanam*!

She starts running in slow motion.

And I pretend like Buddy's watching me, like he can't take his eyes off me, and all the desert people are looking at how beautiful I am, but I don't realize how beautiful I am because I'm having too much fun . . . RUNNING!

A referee whistle tears through the desert fantasy. MEENA *looks around and finds herself back in the high-school gym class.*

So we're doing this dance component in gym class? And we all had to get into groups and come up with an ensemble dance number. And the best group in the class gets to perform for a school assembly in front of the entire school! I would think that would be incentive . . . NOT to do a good job. I got put in the same group as Candice Paskis and her friends? Which is kind of cool . . . And Candice wants to do this "Indian theme" dance and she asked if I could help. Like if I knew anything about Indian dance!

Flashback: MEENA and CANDICE in the girls' change room.

"Um . . . I don't think I do."

Stomp. Stomp.

KALYANI AUNTY is in her basement dance studio.

KALYANI AUNTY: *(on her phone)* GURUMAA-*JI*?! This is too much, TOO MUCH! This gym class asking my girls, my student, to run through their PE hula hoop. They want to teach social study, mathematic, basket-weaving—fine, that being their job—but dance? That Aunty's speciality. They ruining all my student with their Shakira naughty *shame-shame* dancing! I work so hard, for what? ALL WASTE! All stiffness, straightness, *gone!* If they want to learn dance, ask

Aunty! Aunty teach them! <*tsk*> Aunty cool, Aunty bad . . . <*tsk*>
I say Aunty BAD!

Stomp.

KALYANI AUNTY hangs up the phone and exits.

*Halloween. MEENA grabs a bowl of candy that rests by the feet
of the Natraj statue.*

MEENA: So this year for Halloween, I was rehearsing "Nimbooda"—
the Lemon-Lime Lover Dance—late at Kalyani Aunty's house.
MAN! She should've just turned out the lights and pretended not
to be home!

*We hear a doorbell. KALYANI AUNTY eagerly answers the door
and greets a batch of trick-or-treaters.*

KALYANI AUNTY: Hallo! What you supposed to be? Clown? Look
like hermaphrodite to me. Well, here, take some rice. No-no! Take
MORE rice! No, see, in India we give any beggar child who come
to door fistful of RICE. And you have little baby hand, can't take
so much rice! Take more rice. Take it. No, see. Rice? Perfect for
BEGGAR CHILDREN. Even little bit of rice, expand in water, even
more in tummy, you eat for whole week! <*tsk*> Shame-shame on
your parent for no making enough money. Make you go dress like
hermaphrodite from door-to-door in front of whole of neighbour-
hood . . . Meena! Get hermaphrodite baby more rice!

MEENA speaks to her audience in KALYANI AUNTY's foyer.

MEENA: And she makes me hand this stuff out! Like I don't even live here; people are gonna think I support this sort of thing! I mean, not even the shame of being the only house that doesn't hand out chocolate. Not even THAT house that hands out raisins. No, no. That *freak house* that hands out fistfuls of uncooked Basmati rice?! What are those kids going to do with all that rice? See? This is why I want Buddy to just fall in love with me and take me away from all of this!

> *MEENA looks over her shoulder to see if KALYANI AUNTY has overheard, but spots the Natraj statue instead. MEENA averts her eyes and carefully walks outside and closes the door behind her.*

Okay, I've been trying to tell Kalyani Aunty about NOT doing the dance competition, but I can't seem to find the right chance . . .

> *MEENA walks back in through KALYANI AUNTY's front door and closes it.*

Stomp. Stomp.

*On the other side of the door is Vancouver's famous Punjabi
Market at Main Street and 49th.* KALYANI AUNTY *is waiting
for* MEENA *in one of the market fabric stores.*

KALYANI AUNTY examines a sample of chiffon fabric.

KALYANI AUNTY: Meena! Hurry up, we have lot of shopping to do!
Have to pick material for dance costume then rehearse "Nimbooda"
dance. Competition only six months away—

KALYANI AUNTY sees Cal Uncle.

Namaste. Haan-haan, thhik hai! THHIK hai-thhik hai!

She turns back to MEENA.

Oh God, it's that Cal *Uncle* fellow again. Don't look! Always
squinting-squinting. He just trying to see what colour bra I wearing under sari!

To Cal Uncle.

Haan, thik hai, THIK HAI, Cal Uncle.

Back to MEENA.

You know I ask him once, "What your name short for?" You know
what his name? Calendar! You know! January, February, August,
Calendar! Uff! Just show you what class he comes from. *Chalo,* let's
go before he try to treat me to some Thums Up cola again.

MEENA: Try? You downed five bottles last time!

KALYANI AUNTY: I no want to be rude! If I didn't drink *something*, it be slap in his face!

MEENA: You ordered a side of tandoori chicken!

KALYANI AUNTY: You can't have Thums Up without some savoury dish!

MEENA: Why don't you just admit you like him a little bit?

KALYANI AUNTY: <*tsk*> I too old for all this nonsense garbage!

To Cal Uncle.

No, Cal Uncle. I like the colour. I like the colour! But I need to sleep on it! You know, sleeping-sleeping, buying-buying, later-later. Oh I know you have best price in town! You don't have to tell me! HA HA HA!

She whispers to MEENA.

MEENA, let's go.

They get out of the fabric store and end up outside on Main Street, ready to run more errands, when KALYANI AUNTY is distracted.

You hear that? SHHH!

She spots the source.

White people here at big mango sale?

KALYANI AUNTY flaps and waves her hands while hissing and shooing in the direction of an unassuming white family at a local Indian grocery store. The white family are more amazed by the great deal on mangos and don't notice her. KALYANI AUNTY gives up shooing them away.

Busiest day at Indian market and these greedy white folk come and take all of mango for themself?! Make me so angry!!

She takes a moment to collect herself.

You know how many places British colonize? Seventy-seven! Seventy-seven in whole of the world, Meena! They have so much land, so MUCH OF LAND, then be giving us generous gift: two blocks of East Main Street?! Oh thank you, *thank you*, British Raj! No, we follow Gandhi-*ji*'s zero-co-operation movement; I go sit on mango crate and not be getting off from there!

KALYANI AUNTY storms over to the Indian grocery store, leaving MEENA to keep herself occupied.

MEENA: *(to her audience, about to walk off)* That should keep her busy for a while—

MEENA spots someone in the distance and stops in her tracks.

Buddy? Buddy Cain? Buddy Cain in our Punjabi Market!

MEENA smooths her hair, collects herself, and then goes to wave to BUDDY.

Buddy! . . .

MEENA drops her hand as she sees something transpire in the distance. MEENA realizes she's crying and quickly walks away. She spots KALYANI AUNTY and walks over to her.

Kalyani Aunty, can you get off that mango crate? It's nothing; can you just drive me back to Port Moody please? I don't feel very good. No, it's not anything. No, it's really not anything. I just need to go home. No. No . . . no it's not dysentery—can we just go please? I really just want to go to the car . . . and I *don't* want to talk about— Kalyani Aunty! Okay, okay, okay, okay, OKAY! It's . . . Buddy! Buddy Cain's here with Candice Paskis and they were kiss—

Beat.

Stomp.

KALYANI AUNTY: Wait-wait? MORE white people? Come on, man!

KALYANI AUNTY hisses and shoos in the direction of BUDDY and CANDICE.

Stomp.

MEENA: . . . And Candice was wearing this dot on her forehead and she had all this henna on her hands! And you know how I feel about white people wearing henna! Why don't you people understand those HERBS weren't meant for your skin type! You just look like-like a CROSS! Between jaundice and leprosy, leprosy and jaundice—

Stomp.

KALYANI AUNTY: White peopla wearing *our* henna? Aunty count to ten: one *patak-masala*, two *patak-masala*, three *patak-masala* . . . <*tsk*> Meena-*beta*, just calm down, okay?

Stomp.

MEENA: You just don't get it! I could never compete with a girl like Candice Paskis! Skinny and pretty and BLOND! . . .

Stomp.

KALYANI AUNTY: You think I don't know? In India, there was British architect stationed in village, Victor, but I call him Vicky. Handsome, like John Ritter, but smart like Lord Krishna. It not even enter my mind that such handsome, important man be thinking of me this way. And all of village know he had rich white girl back in England. He watch my dance practice. One day I tell him if you be watching you must be learning also. You should have seen his lotus flower! *Arey*, hopeless flower! I laughed so hard, so hard!

Then he kiss me. So scared! Thought I was pregnant? But Vicky laugh. Say that not how you have baby. Then I thought for sure he must be leaving white girl and be marrying me, but then white girl come to India. Blond hair, short cut! Skinny-skinny like pencil, holding Vicky's hand in front of my face. Well, I tell Vicky, you send blondie home, we go to get married. He say, yeah okay, you meet me at train station and we go. I wait, he no come. I go home, he no come. Vicky get transfer to England and marry blondie. You know, these white boy just plain stupid, but white girl? Thief, Meena, thief! See how she steal from Kalyani Aunty?

Stomp.

MEENA: We lose at everything! No! Like cricket! And soccer! *The Academy Awards*! We can't even make it into the Olympics! Sure we dance great dances, but that's because no one else knows about them so they can't show us how to do it any better!

Stomp.

KALYANI AUNTY: EH? Indian girl, Indian dancer do anything—even get white boy! Can this Candice Pakistan do "Nimbooda"? No fucking way, blondie! This time three's being a CROWD!

Stomp.

MEENA: GOD! So much for Grad 2013! This was suppose to be *my* summer! The Summer of Meena and Buddy!

Stomp.

KALYANI AUNTY: I'm sorry, hold the phone. Summer of Meena and Buddy? What about Summer of Meena and Kalyani Aunty? Hello? You forget dance comeptition or what?

Stomp.

MEENA: Do I look like I care about a stupid, waste-of-time dance competition? God, think about somebody else for a change!

Stomp.

KALYANI AUNTY: Meena—

Stomp.

MEENA: NO! I QUIT! I'M NOT DANCING ANYMORE!! I'M NOT GOING TO STUPID INDIA TO DANCE IN YOUR STUPID DANCE COMPETITION!

Stomp. Beat.

KALYANI AUNTY: Fine. Fine. No, fine. I'll find somebody else. *Chalo*, I drop you home?

Stomp.

MEENA: No. I think I'll just take the bus . . .

A remix of the "Nimbooda" song plays as MEENA walks away down Main Street's Punjabi Market and tries to soak in what's just happened.

KALYANI AUNTY appears next to her Natraj statue in her home. She sits and is tying a ribbon around a gift box for Lalita.

KALYANI AUNTY: First time I see Vicky was at village fair. I wearing red chiffon sari, drinking Thums Up with straw. My mummy-daddy no let me drink Thums Up, forget wearing red chiffon sari, so I had to do in secret. Vicky tell me that red really being my colour. Making me look like real pretty lady. I know, he say that! But such windy day *na*, couldn't control. Not used to wearing sari then! Wear sari for school functions only. Just keep falling off shoulder just like in movie! Oh, but in movie girl no even try to keep on sari. Eh! Always finding excuse to take off! So much of promise. Vicky telling me there lots of Thums Up in England. Much better Thums Up than there being in India. And every day like wedding celebration. Shehnai always playing in street. Always celebrating. And I thinking I being so lucky. To find such good man who just be taking me away.

KALYANI AUNTY looks to the Natraj statue and places the gift box preciously at the statue's feet, the way one would place a Christmas gift under the tree.

MEENA appears with her backpack and approaches her audience.

MEENA: So Kalyani Aunty's pretty mad at me. I asked her what time we were gonna go for our regular trip to the Punjabi Market, but she said she was too busy! No, no. She's *never* too busy. Not for the Punjabi Market! So I tried to make her laugh, or at least yell at me like she usually does. So in dance class everyone's doing this?

She dances an Indian phrase.

But I'm doing THIS!

She does jumping jacks.

. . . But nothing! I don't even know why she's so mad at me. She found a replacement for me . . . Yeah! LALITA!

MEENA makes her body look three times larger with her hands.

LALITA?! The best she could come up with was Lalita? And okay, I know what you're going to say: "Hey, Meena, why do you care? You didn't want to do the stupid dance competition anyways?" But I'm thinking of the quality of the "Nimbooda" dance. No! I don't think it's realistic to choose LALITA to do this top-notch dance competition when-when-when-when . . . Lalita's getting married! YEAH. I thought it was pretty unbelievable at first too, but Lalita's marrying our really hot tabla drummer, Sid. So how's Lalita supposed to focus on making the "Nimbooda" dance really, really good when

Lalita's got this Summer of Lalita and Sid wedding to think about? Whatever. I guess that's none of my business anymore.

> MEENA *turns around and runs into the Natraj statue on her way out. They meet eyes for a moment.* MEENA *decisively turns away and walks through the doors of her high school in Port Moody.*

Just before spring break.

I decided to concentrate on school. Like NO dance, JUST school!

But then . . . our stupid dance got picked for the stupid school assembly! Remember gym class? The "dance ensemble"?

And Candice. Candice Paskis is all like, *(uses an Indian dance hand gesture)* "Hey guys, I came up with some new moves. It's like 'Indian dance'?" Indian?

Uh, hello? I think I might happen to know a little something about "Indian dance."

And then Candice? Candice Paskis, is all like, "Hey guys, I saw John Travolta do this one in *Pulp Fiction*. It's like Aquarius, like the fish-eyes move!"

I'll show you fish eyes! It's actually called *"Kartarimukha."*

> MEENA *demonstrates the bharatanatyam single-hand gesture series in sequence as she speaks.*

It's the fourth *mudra* in a series of single hand gestures used to storytell in pure classical dance. I mean, let's have a little give and take here! First she steals my Buddy, my Grad 2013 date, and then she wants to steal my dance too? She's just a big STEALER!

> MEENA *throws her backpack off in a temper tantrum and then stares at it. Beat. Embarrassed,* MEENA *then opens the backpack and takes out her scrapbook, and opens it to a page of choreography notes across from the Aishwarya Rai movie poster.*

But then I went home. And I started to think about how to make the dance good—well, as good as it can be. And I came back really excited, you know? Because there's this problem spot in the dance that no one else could figure out, but I . . . I actually suggested doing a spin where we all do this!

> MEENA *performs a series of precise spins using the hand gesture for "Nimbooda."*

But Candice Paskis was all like, "Um, I don't think they do THAT in Indian dance."

But then Candice's friends who are usually like her yes-men, right? They said that they never thought I could dance like that. So then I showed them some more stuff.

> *She demonstrates a full Indian dance phrase for the other girls.*

Like easy stuff; stuff I've been doing since I was really little. And they just ate it up! And the best part—the best part was? CANDICE PASKIS? Couldn't say anything because she was the odd one out!

Destiny's Child's "Survivor" begins to play. MEENA is in the centre of the gym in the middle of their school assembly. She performs the first gesture asking for blessings in classical dance and then expertly performs a dance full of spins, intricate hand gestures, and footwork matched to the contemporary beat. MEENA dances with complete confidence and ownership before her high-school peers.

MEENA ends in a triumphant classical Indian pose, stomping her foot as though she has commandèd its finale. The end of the dance brings the high-school audience to their feet, showering MEENA in applause and cheers.

(excitedly) And it was in front of the entire school! Everyone was coming up to me and telling me what a good job I did and how they never thought I could move like that! And Buddy! Buddy Cain comes up to me and he's all like:

MEENA summons BUDDY by channelling the Indian dance pose for "warrior with a bow and arrow."

BUDDY: "Whoa. That was like? That was like . . . really like . . . WHOA. Whoa. You're hair's like . . . really . . . SHINY?!

MEENA: *(to her audience)* EEEEEEEEEEEE!

Beat.

But then Buddy sees Candice and whispers in her ear. He spins her around by her waist and kisses her and calls her his "bitch." And I just feel so stupid . . . STUPID for just . . . standing there. Candice is hanging all over Buddy and tells me I did a really good job. She said that I had really good spirit and I did the moves like a real pro. And she says she really hopes to see me at Grad 2013. Even though she can't remember my name.

Stomp.

MEENA disappears as KALYANI AUNTY reappears in her basement dance studio speaking to her students.

KALYANI AUNTY: Sometimes I be thinking what it looking like when Vicky kissed this blondie girl. In beginning I think they no be together like that, like just wave hello/goodbye, nothing else. So simple I was being then. Then I really start thinking what it being like when they be married couple . . . sharing bed, touching skin, being loving . . . But nothing prepare you like seeing it real life. When I see Vicky put arm around blondie, whole of his hand on her back, rubbing, stroking like he really be loving-caring for her? Looking at her like nobody else exist? I feel whole heart just crack in chest. Thinking if this what they doing in public, just think what happening behind closed door? Make me feel real crappy. Feel like no be able to stand no more. Asking myself, "How I keep going on? Just like nothing happen?"

Stomp.

MEENA arrives again but hides behind the picture of Aishwarya Rai on the front of her scrapbook.

MEENA: So it's like a month away till Grad . . .

. . . and I don't even want to go. But I already bought my tight red dress—with shoes—and it was really expensive, so I have to go. I don't even have a date! OH! But Lalita's got a date! A DATE TO GET MARRIED!

> *"Balle Balle" from the film* Bride & Prejudice *starts playing and* MEENA *arrives at Lalita's in-home bridal shower.* MEENA *lays out Lalita's gift boxes as she dresses in a costume that makes her look like the son of a Punjabi farmer with an oversized shirt, turban, and large moustache.* MEENA *dances with abandon and masculinity, yet she is clearly still a skilled dancer and retains a dancer's grace despite her ridiculous getup. The song continues to underscore the scene, but* MEENA *takes off her costume as she prepares for the next phase of Lalita's bridal shower.*

(to her audience) So it's Lalita's "bachlorette/ladies party." It's this big party where all the girls get together to sing and dance and put on henna! Like give the bride a really proper send-off. We're having the party early because there won't be any time when she gets back from India. And all the girls are here! Like Sukhi and Pavan . . . and Kalyani Aunty's here with all the other aunties, but they're drinking all this spiked Thums Up! . . .

> *Stomp.*

> KALYANI AUNTY, *drunk, arrives but is unsure of where she is. She spots* LALITA *in a corner of the party and remembers where she is and why.*

KALYANI AUNTY: LALITA! LALITA! Come here! Talk to Aunty; we have friendly chat! So you be knowing about bird and bee or what? Well, have to know! Getting married! Good-looking man have wandering eye! So you USE dance! KEEP Sid! Don't worry! Aunty show you! Here, hold this.

KALYANI AUNTY uses classical Indian dance poses to narrate her mythical foreplay.

See, I'm waiting, waiting, looking so . . . *<tsk>* SO BEAUTIFUL! Then HE come.

Her right hand grabs her left wrist.

AHHH! Krishna, NO! Bad. Very, very BAD Krishna. You can LOOK, but you cannot *touch*. Oh Krishna. You're such a *naughty* Krishna. How can I say no to you? Big blue body! Why don't I blow on your flute?

KALYANI AUNTY performs the gesture for Krishna playing his flute with her hands and then blows hard into her hands. She grabs her own wrist again.

Ouch! Krishna! Let go, *na*! Oh, Krishna! Forbidden fruit is always sweetest! KRISHNA!

She embraces herself with her back turned to the audience. MEENA emerges to speak to Lalita.

MEENA: Hey, Lalita! Oh, I'm really glad you liked the dance . . . Yeah it was pretty funny with the moustache. I think it's really great you have like a date for life now! I mean, you and Sid are going to go to Grad 2013 together, right?

Great! Hmm? Yeah. Yeah, I heard. Yeah, you're taking my place in the dance competition, but . . . okay. I don't want to scare you, but I think you should know. India? Isn't like it is in the movies! No! Everyone's not all dressed up nice and dancing in the streets! No! Everyone's starving and poor. Oh! No! I totally don't want to scare you, but I just thought you should know there're like DEAD BODIES . . . lying in the streets! Just LYING there! So you be careful you don't catch like . . . *avian bird flu* or something! Because there are these DEAD BODIES just lying there—

> *KALYANI AUNTY appears, having overheard their whole conversation, and intervenes.*

> *Stomp.*

KALYANI AUNTY: HEH? Don't listen to this nonsense, Lalita. No dead bodies in India!

> *Stomp.*

MEENA: What about all those people lying on the side of the road?

> *Stomp.*

KALYANI AUNTY: It like that here, Meena. You feel tired, you sleep wherever, on side of road, WHEREVER.

> *Stomp.*

MEENA: You know, Lalita, I heard India has the PLAGUE! That's why I got you this.

MEENA pulls out a medical mask. KALYANI AUNTY quickly grabs it from her.

Stomp. Stomp.

KALYANI AUNTY: Give me that!

She snatches the mask from MEENA.

No plague in India! Zero plague in India!

Stomp. Stomp. MEENA grabs the medical mask back.

MEENA: I think India has a little bit of plague. I mean, it's so dirty . . .

Stomp. Stomp. KALYANI AUNTY grabs the medical mask back.

KALYANI AUNTY: No such thing as getting "little bit" of plague. Biggest epidemic of plague where it happen? Europe! Pure, clean England get plague because they so dirty—so DIRTY—but then try to cover dirt smell with perfume from France, so France get plague! Then France be needing some schnitzel sausage or some garbage like that. Austria-Germany get plague. And it keep happening like that—somebody need windmill—WINDMILL? Holland get plague. Somebody need big, funny-looking hat? Spain get plague. Dirty England always *infecting* and then—THEN saying *(in bad British accent)*, "Oh, India is so dirty. Let's have some tea." If India being dirty, it being your fault. YOU MAKE INDIA DIRTY!

She throws the mask to the ground.

LALITA! Go get Aunty paper map of England! I want to tear into shreds and shreds!

She makes a paper-shredding gesture with her hands.

Stomp. Stomp.

MEENA points to the mask.

MEENA: Yeah, Lalita, I think you should take the mask just in case?

Stomp. Stomp.

KALYANI AUNTY: STEP AWAY FROM THE MASK, LALITA. STEP AWAY— put down that KFC. Put it down! Okay, this being your party, you go be social. Yeah! Go, be social.

She watches Lalita exit before turning to MEENA.

Meenakshi. You no want to go to India, to dance, I no say nothing, but you no ruin this for Lalita. You act like you no like India, go after some white boy, then feeling sorry for yourself, but people still see what you really are, and right now? I see you? Selfish bitch!

Stomp. Stomp. KALYANI AUNTY performs a dance hand gesture waving over her face so she disappears and MEENA appears in her place. Beat.

MEENA: You can see I'm trying here, right? I mean, here I am passing this olive branch to Kalyani Aunty, but Kalyani Aunty? She's just stomping on it and chewing off the olives and spitting out the pits. But she's spitting the pits in my face, and then one of the pits gets in my eye and I'm like, "I got pits in my eyes!" Okay. I guess I'm just a little mad right now, but not in a way that's anybody else's fault except my own. 'Cause I finally see that for all this time Buddy existed for me? I never existed to Buddy. Not ever. Like him dressing up like an Indian cowboy? Chasing me down the beach? Wooing me through song . . . and dance? That never happened. That was just me. Because while I was thinking all that, Buddy was with Candice. After school, in her bedroom, touching her face, stroking the hair away from her face, kissing—

Like how do I keep doing this, right? Like how do I keep breaking my own heart?

Stomp.

MEENA dances into a jump and disappears as KALYANI AUNTY lands in her place. She is in the middle of the aftermath of Lalita's bridal shower.

KALYANI AUNTY: You know, I almost get married. Gurumaa-*ji* help my parent fix up my marriage. Had to dance for him. Dance being only thing I knowing how to do, but dance enough. When marriage date fixed, I no complain. Everything I see, smell, all reminding me of Vicky, and this guy talk big. Talk like Amreekan, live in US, so I thought I just go and forget. Then on wedding day? I looking so beautiful with red veil, sitting, waiting in front of priest, shehnai band ringing in my ear so loud. Then finally groom arrive. On big white horse with all guest following, but when he get down he slip on something, fall, no open eye, have to rush him to hospital. And everyone saying, "Bad omen! Kalyani at fault! Must be bad bride!" What bad bride? YOU BAD BRIDE! He get little cut on lip, nothing else, just little cut— They call whole thing off. He marry some other girl, take some other girl away. Well, so what? SO WHAT? I no want to marry such stupid man anyway! So accident-prone! "LOOK where you're stepping, *na*?" Stupid . . . ASSHOLE.

KALYANI AUNTY's cellphone rings.

Stomp.

Haan, Gurumaa-*ji*? . . . Yeah, yeah, Lalita. Have her ladies party. What the hell she was wearing? Look like big diaper! Big trash-bag diaper! Meena?

Moves away out of earshot.

You should have seen Meena dance! Dress like boy, like Punjabi! Making me laugh just thinking about it. And all by herself she make it up! Expression, posture . . . <*tsk*> just too good! But then look at her teacher. *Haan*, what else you expect? Only best you can accept!

Stomp.

KALYANI AUNTY hangs up the phone and turns to leave. MEENA appears behind her. She makes the Indian dance gesture for "one with eyes like a fish."

MEENA: *(to her audience)* Grad . . . 2013! Hit it!

MEENA points to the stage manager. "Get Ur Freak On" plays; Grad 2013 is here. MEENA gets ready for the dance by slipping into a pair of red shoes. She finds a wrist corsage at the feet of the Natraj statue and dips her wrist into it. MEENA arrives in her red dress at her dimly lit high-school gym covered in South Asian themed decorations. She looks around and is not impressed.

(to her audience) So this grad sucks dick. Grad was SUPPOSED to be downtown Vancouver, but instead it's in the Port Moody Senior Secondary gym. Candice Paskis was head of the grad committee. She came up with this Starlight Taj Mahal theme, so everyone's dressed the way I am ALL YEAR ROUND! Like a bindi . . . or a henna tattoo . . . or some weird scarf in colours no Indian person would be caught dead wearing?

And if that isn't bad enough? Sukhi and Pavan brought dates! Like everyone's here with a date except me . . . Oh, well, EXCEPT Kalyani Aunty, but she's just here chaperoning Lalita and Sid, who keep staring at each other like nobody else is in the room.

Destiny's Child's "Survivor" begins to play. MEENA *looks to the speakers.*

IS THAT "Survivor"?! CANDICE!

That's when I go out to the parking lot for some air!

MEENA arrives in the high school's Top Lot parking lot in her red high-heeled shoes.

But I accidentally see Candice and Buddy and they're fighting and crying. Well, Candice is fighting and Buddy's crying?

MEENA uses Indian dance hand gestures to represent CANDICE *and* BUDDY.

Candice is all like, "I'm going and that's that."

And then Buddy's all like, "But you don't even know anything about Indian dance!"

And Candice is like, "Yeah I do, remember the 'Fish Eyes' dance I choreographed for the school?"

And I'm like, "FUCK YOU, CANDICE!"

I say that in my head, right?

And then Buddy's like, "But you're my bitch! You can't go do Indian dance!"

But then Candice says, "I'm sorry your feelings are hurt, but I'm going to England, and I'm going to the Coventry School of Bhangra, and I'm sorry you're obviously way more into me than I'm into you."

MEENA watches CANDICE go back into the gym.

And she just leaves him there crying, like SOBBING! And I can't just leave him there. We *do* have a history together! I can't leave the man I might have married—I might marry! . . .

MEENA approaches BUDDY, who is hunched over his car, sobbing.

HEY, BUDDY! Hi! We were in Socials together . . . my name's Meena; it's short for Meenakshi—it means Fish . . . Eyes . . . Whatever. I accidentally overheard you and Candice fighting and—oh God. Please stop crying. You gotta stop crying. I mean I know how much it hurts right now, but it'll go away . . . YEAH! IT'LL GO AWAY—well, not right now . . . I mean later, it'll go away—later . . . Okay, you gotta stop crying! Okay, I'm just going to say it. I'm gonna put it out there. You're too good for Candice! We all know it! You're just so wonderful and great and you have no idea how many girls would love to be with you . . . STOP . . . CRYING. I mean . . . do you want to see a dance?

MEENA dances a shorter version of the "Nimbooda" in her high-heel shoes. She is transported to every Aishwarya Rai movie she has ever seen as she dances. She dances as though she is finally performing for her intended audience for the first time. Just as she lands in the triumphant last posture of the dance:

I LOVE YOU! YOU'RE MY LEMON-LIME LOVER.

Did you want to maybe go inside? And slow dance?! What? Oh.

No, that's okay. NO! That's fine! Totally! I mean, thank you—sorry, thank you? Oh! For the dance! Well, you're welcome for the dance. I feel really good about that right now . . . Hmm? What am I doing for the summer? I got a couple of projects . . . like, like . . . Dance stuff. What-what-what-what are you doing . . . for the summer? Waiting for Candice. Well wow! Waiting for Candice! Well, good luck waiting for Candice . . . BITCH!

"Jai Ho!," a Pussycat Dolls remix, plays inside the gym. MEENA walks back to the dance.

So National India Day's still going on inside. And Candice Paskis is Indian lap-dancing for Dubee—

"(I've Had) The Time of My Life" from the film Dirty Dancing *plays, and the already dim lights get darker, setting a cheesy romantic mood. A disco ball begins to spin and its light spills its sequins onto* MEENA. MEENA *shrinks with embarrassment.*

—and everyone's dancing with their dates! Like Lalita and Sid look like they're having a really good time together, and everyone's just DANCING with their dates! Oh, okay. Except Kalyani Aunty, but she's just off in the corner and she looks kinda mad?

MEENA approaches KALYANI AUNTY.

Kalyani Aunty?

Stomp stomp. Stomp.

KALYANI AUNTY appears out of the shadows of the gym.

KALYANI AUNTY: Do you see this fatty-fatty-fat-fat Lalita? What the hell she's wearing? So much flashy-flashy for graduation dance, just think how she'll be looking as bride? Sid go blind!

Stomp stomp. Stomp.

MEENA: I don't think Sid cares because he keeps staring at Lalita like nobody else is in the room. And Sid makes Lalita really, really happy.

Stomp stomp. Stomp.

KALYANI AUNTY: Of course she happy, she just screw over Aunty!

Madame Lalita decide she no go to India. Say that Sid no like her dancing in public. That if she dance, she should dance for him only. Phht! Like anyone breaking down door to watch Lalita dance. What the hell I'm going to do? Everyone expecting something from Aunty! Oh and Gurumaa-*ji*. Gurumaa-*ji* always saying, "Good girl, good dancer only be coming from India." But I want to show that, no, girl from here just as good as from there, that Aunty no waste time.

Stomp stomp. Stomp.

MEENA: Do you still have my travel visa for India?

Stomp stomp. Stomp.

KALYANI AUNTY: Why, you want to go to India? To dance? You yanking on Aunty's chain or what? What happened to Summer of Meena and Buddy?

Stomp stomp. Stomp.

MEENA: I don't want Buddy. Anyways, I think I can do the "Nimbooda" dance really, really good.

Stomp stomp . Stomp.

KALYANI AUNTY: Oh, Meena. Aunty tell you story, huh?

Stomp stomp. Stomp.

MEENA: Can you save it? I'm really tired . . .

Stomp stomp. Stomp.

KALYANI AUNTY: AUNTY SAY SHE TELL YOU *STORY*!

KAYLANI AUNTY sits down but is suddenly transported to her basement dance studio. She sits in the same place she did at the beginning of the play and uses the same Indian hand-gesture series she used at the top of the show.

See. Poor fisherman go home to his beautiful wife and say, "Not one single edible fish left in river! Only fish I find was this one! With red eye! Skin so oily, but eyes good! You'll get at least six gold pieces at market."

Fisherman's beautiful wife about to cut, but then great voice come from fish. "Please! I beg you! Don't cut me up!"

Fisherman's beautiful wife ask, "How can you be happy being so undesirable?"

Fish say, "I not be happy if I was desired, because then my life would be much shorter. See. I no look like other fishes. All fishermen throw me back into river because I so 'undesirable.' So I keep swimming, keep seeing new parts of river. Please. Let this useless creature live happy in river!"

Fisherman's beautiful wife look into fish eye. Then that night she run to the riverside with fish and look at her reflection in water. She looked at her beautiful locks of hair, her moon-shape face, and feel empty inside. But then! Look at fish with oily skin and red eye? And feel *joy* like she never feel before. Fisherman's beautiful wife

look back at house, but then, *suddenly*, find herself turned into fish!
Swimming in river! Swimming . . . right next to fish? With red eye.

*KALYANI AUNTY ends the story with the gesture for "one with
eyes like a fish."*

End of play.

BOYS WITH CARS

Boys With Cars was commissioned, developed, and produced by Nightswimming and premiered in a double bill with *Fish Eyes* at the Great Canadian Theatre Company, Ottawa, on October 16, 2014, with the following cast and creative team:

Choreographer and actor: Anita Majumdar
Director and dramaturg: Brian Quirt
Producer: Rupal Shah
Stage manager: Sandy Plunkett
Lighting design: Rebecca Picherack
Set and costume design: Jackie Chau
Sound design: Christopher Stanton
Production manager: Simon Rossiter

Characters

Naznin
Gustakhi
Lucky
Buddy
Candice
Miss Flemming
Mr. Peter Nicholas Smyth

*In the dark, Imran Khan's "Amplifier" plays. Two headlights
appear and the spill of light reveals* NAZ *standing on the roof
of a red Mini Cooper. The lights of the parking lot show* NAZ
*in detail; she's dressed like a Mughal courtesan in a glittering
peacock-blue Indian dance skirt and Indian jewellery, all covered by a hoodie. On the roof of the car,* NAZ *dances a full-body
version of the Fisherperson Story from* Fish Eyes. *Her dance
retains a traditional grace, but is distinctly sharp and vengeful.
A fury pulses through* NAZ, *and yet with every spin her skirt*

flares upwards, and for a moment she appears like a shimmering teardrop. By the end of the dance she notices she is being watched and immediately stops dancing. She quickly sits down on the roof of the Mini Cooper with her back turned to the audience and shades her face with her hand.

Present: May 2014, Victoria Day weekend.

Noises from a nearby reception are heard. NAZ *notices her watcher hasn't left yet.* NAZ *fiddles with her iPod earbuds and puts one in her left ear. Chris Brown's "Kiss Kiss" underscores.*

NAZ: I have this thing where I listen to the same song over and over again. I'll be listening to that song when something kinda big's happening in my life, but then I'll stop listening to it, but then I'll hear it again and all of it . . .

She listens for a moment.

. . . comes back again . . . So I try not to listen to those songs anymore.

NAZ *takes the earbud from her ear. "Kiss Kiss" stops playing.*

People get mad when I say I like Chris Brown . . .

She rolls her eyes.

. . . because he hit Rihanna. People don't get there's two sides to every story. Chris is really sorry . . . and HOT. And he's making it all about the music now, so I don't know why people don't just get over themselves, so . . .

You here for the wedding tonight? Well duh, right? Are you with the bride or the groom? Yeah, me too.

Gustakhi's supposed to be here by now. Oh, yeah, she's looking for parking. Did YOU have to look for parking? Of course not, because this school has more parking spots than it does textbooks. Gustakhi was supposed to be here ten minutes ago. We're the dance company for tonight. I love dancing . . . except for the part where people have to look at me. At every one of these things, I dance-dance-dance, the crowd watches me, and for a split second I think he might be there. "I don't even want to see him!" I say that to trick God.

She holds up an Allah pendant hanging around her neck.

Because *God's* always giving me the opposite of what I want. And then I wonder when he's coming back, because he HAS to come back, right . . . ? My dance set's pretty easy; dance *Slumdog Millionaire* songs for white-people weddings.

> *"Jai Ho!" from* Slumdog Millionaire *plays.* NAZ *dances on the roof of the Mini Cooper, lightly kicking up her feet and putting graceful attention into her hips. In the middle of an intricate Indian hand gesture,* NAZ *turns the song off abruptly.*

Fucking "Jai Ho!" Sorry, but I really hate that song. It's like the Le Château national anthem, and other AWESOME stores like that. When I first started performing weddings, it was all like:

> *"Jai Ho!" plays from the beginning again.* NAZ *dances to the same choreography as earlier and exaggerates her enthusiasm for the dance. She abruptly turns off the song at the same place as before.*

But one year later it's more like:

> *"Jai Ho!" plays from the beginning again.* NAZ's *eyes widen and she dances like she's being held hostage by the Russian militia. The song abruptly stops again.*

I practice here in the school parking lot. It's the only square footage in Port Moody that's mine . . . and it isn't even. Not the car, not the lot. I don't even have a licence to drive myself out of here. You think

Port Moody's *nice*? Port Moody has this inlet of water, mountains, trees, but do you notice any of that? Nope. You look at the motherfucking stacks of the YELLOWEST sulfur—UNSECURED—piled up over there on the Barnet Highway! Speaking of acidic compounds, where's Gustakhi?! She's not my mom. She's like my *Toddlers & Tiaras* show mom, so not like a mom who loves me or anything? I don't have parents. I mean, I HAVE parents, but not ones I can see in front of my face. And no, I'm not like the grade-twelve girls who lie about having dead parents to be deep and not wash their hair. I live with Gustakhi. And work with Gustakhi.

Flashback: GUSTAKHI appears in her home.

GUSTAKHI: We're like a *Mughal-e-Azam* courtesan business, Naznin; you dance for the whites, I keep their dollars. Just like old-time India . . . before England showed up and gave us AIDS.

Present: NAZ sits down on the roof of the Mini Cooper.

NAZ: Our usual gigs are in Vancouver. After driving us back to Port Moody, Gustakhi helps me out of my costume because the hooks are at the back.

NAZ tries to unhook the back of her blouse but can't reach. Flashback: GUSTAKHI appears and sits behind NAZ, undoing the hooks of the blouse from behind.

GUSTAKHI: If only you wore all your clothing with buttons in the back, Naznin. Then it wouldn't be so easy to take it off for every boy who offered you a bag of Timbits!

Present: NAZ dangles her feet off the roof of the car.

NAZ: Gustakhi's not a dancer. She's barely HUMAN most of the time. But I keep living with her and she keeps letting me . . . as long as I keep dancing. She moved here from Punjab after her kids died. After high school ended, I needed a new place to live and work . . . I met Gustakhi at the mall and we really hit it off—

Flashback: June 2013. NAZ approaches GUSTAKHI in the Coquitlam Centre parking lot.

Hi, *Aunty*—

GUSTAKHI: Don't do that; I hate that. All you Indian kids, I don't know who told you every person you meet on the road to turn them into family. I'm not your family.

NAZ: Sorry, *Aunty*, or, um—

GUSTAKHI: Eh! You look like a giraffe. What's wrong with you? How come you stand so tall? You look like you're proud of yourself.

NAZ: I'm not proud. I'm an Indian dancer, so—

GUSTAKHI: Eh! You see this Shanta Claush operation over here in the food court? Huh! Christmas in July! What a pile of horseshit! So any time is the right time to teach small girls if you want nice things, just sit in an old man's lap?! Every year I enter His temple at the Coquitlam Centre Mall Centre and I say, "Shanta-*ji*, please. Make this life a little easier . . . with a new samosa maker . . . and a bigger mirror. I can't see myself properly in my one at home!" But *Shanta's* a regular Sherry Seinfeld: "Well maybe if you ate less samosa you fit into existing mirror"—"Ha ha ha"?! And then his *kameeni* Mrs. Claush says it's little Suzy's turn. So I told little Suzy,

"YOU WAIT YOUR TURN, LITTLE SUZY!" You're a girl; get used to being served last from now, only!

Back to the present.

NAZ: *(points to the car)* This? Is Lucky's car. Lucky Punjabi? He's my boyfriend. He's coming back for the wedding tonight. When we were still in school, Lucky'd park in Top Lot parking along with the other "cools" from our school. Middle Lot's teacher parking and Bottom Lot's for the rest of the kingdom. This car is like Lucky's religion . . .

Flashback: One week before the Victoria Day weekend, May 2014. GUSTAKHI, in her living room, approaches NAZ.

GUSTAKHI: What happened to Lucky Punjabi? Did Calgary "stampede" our Lucky out of town? You never told me that part of the story, Naznin.

Present: GUSTAKHI is nowhere to be seen but NAZ, rattled, looks to see if she's arrived.

NAZ: Port Moody Senior Secondary. PMSS for short. Oh, I suggested alternate names. Like name it after Albert Street down the hill: *ASSS*? But Principal Shaker said I was in enough trouble and mature PMSS girls should know better.

I'm not nervous. I never get nervous. I mean, the last time I felt like *this* was . . . Golden Spike Fest 2012.

Ever since July 1886, Port Moody celebrates trains stopping in Port Moody—*on purpose*—by watching locals perform by day and teens

ODing on drugs by night. My dance teacher forced me to do this
Indian dance—

> *NAZ demonstrates a version of the Natraj statue pose with the
> hand gesture for "one with eyes like a fish" by her left eye.*

—which got seen by a ton of the "cools" from my school. None of
them even knew my name. How could they, they never saw me. But
now these guys parked their SUVs around Rocky Point stage and
pressed their eyes into me while licking ice cream cones.

> *Flashback: Golden Spike Days Festival, July 2012. NAZ per-
> forms a classical dance to the song "Laal Ishq" from the film*
> Goliyon Ki Raasleela Ram-Leela *on a makeshift stage in the
> middle of the park. In between quick spins and angular arm
> movements lies an entrancing softness. NAZ's genuine joy for the
> dance bursts from her and pulls the watcher's gaze even closer.
> NAZ ends in a traditional Kathak/North Indian dance posture*

that demurely hides her face. Upon the end of the dance, NAZ
turns away from the audience and looks down.

(avoiding eye contact) I get off stage and I look down because if I
can't see them, they can't see me, right? But then I feel someone
coming up to me; Buddy Cain and me meet eyes as he walks over
with Candice Paskis trying to catch up behind him in her red bikini
and cowboy hat, until, thank God—

Akon's "Chammak Challo" plays. NAZ *turns sharply.* LUCKY
*Punjabi appears on the Golden Spike Festival stage and dances
like a sincere but mediocre* America's Got Talent *contestant.
But what* LUCKY *lacks in dance skills, he makes up for in self-as-
sured bravado. The song ends and* LUCKY *addresses his public
while noticing* NAZ *standing in the crowd.*

LUCKY: Name's LUCKY PUN-
JABI! And I'll be signing
autographs by Pajo's
Fish & Chip Hut with
my bro from another
ho, Buddy Cain. YEAH,
BUDDY!

   *LUCKY sees NAZ
   trying to leave.*

Hey . . . Oh . . .
no . . . what have
I done? I've Axe
Body Sprayed-a-
nated myself. For

the fans. Ladies. Love it. Hey, Naznin! Did you know I am a founding member of the Coventry School of Bhangra? Yeah! I invented the "Bhangra burpee." You know?

> *LUCKY dances a Bhangra move while hopping on one leg and pumping his arms in the air. He then pounces to the ground into a push-up and jumps back up.*

BURPEE! Naznin, yeah? Pretty good back there. I love watching your hands.

> *NAZ shouts over the crowd, looking up at LUCKY on the stage.*

NAZ: *(shouting, looking up)* Everyone has hands.

LUCKY: You Indian dance pretty good, Naznin.

> *LUCKY appears to leave nonchalantly but then immediately turns back to NAZ and takes out a Keg Steakhouse mint.*

It's from the Keg. The steakhouse? It's my "Lucky Keg mint," but I want you to hold it for me because that's how good you dance.

NAZ: *(to wedding guest)* Lucky says he's moving to PMSS in the fall and that I should remember the name:

LUCKY: LUCKY PUNJABI!

He does his dance move again.

BURPEE!

> *LUCKY throws the Keg mint into the air and NAZ picks it up.*
> *The Pussycat Dolls's remix of "Jai Ho!" plays as NAZ looks at the*
> *mint for a moment, then dances with genuine enthusiasm to*
> *the song. NAZ spins into the first day of grade twelve at PMSS,*
> *September 2012. MISS FLEMMING appears in the PMSS gym.*

MISS FLEMMING blows on a whistle while bouncing a basketball.

MISS FLEMMING: All right, girls, let's kick off Miss Flemming's Gym
12 by getting sex-ed done and out of the way! But keep dribbling
your balls: NO WATER! Now, I've heard a lot of you doe-eyed gazelles
talkin' about date rape—PASS!

She passes her basketball to one of the girls.

Rape is a two-way street, ladies. When you decide to kiss a guy for a certain amount of time and then you stop because you "changed your mind," well, that poor guy's gonna get blue balls. *Blue balls*— PASS—is where a guy needs to release the stress *you* caused him. If a deer gets hit by a car, well what was the deer doing in the middle of the street? At night? BY HERSELF? So girls who get date raped just rape themselves. Girls? Man up, and let's end date rape forever!

MISS FLEMMING holds her basketball and starts nodding and clapping loudly.

Woo! Yeah! PASS!

MR. PETER NICHOLAS SMYTH appears and addresses his classroom.

MR. PETER NICHOLAS SMYTH: All right, ladies and gents, welcome to this year's English 12. I'm your "commando" in chief, Mr. Peter Nicholas Smyth, but you can call me P-N-S, P-N-S, P-N-S, P-N-S, P-N-S, P-N-S, P-N-S— Say it real fast and what do you got? You got penis! Now we're going to start off with *Mother Courage*, or as they say in the theatre—

He acts out the famed Mother Courage *silent-screaming gesture.*

"Silent-scream," that's what I was doing there—silent scream our way through *Mother Courage*. God. What a bitch. Am I right, gents in the back? But don't worry, everyone gets to read the screenplay I wrote this summer: *The Never-Ending Story: My 5 Seasons on* MacGyver. Working title. Now it won't be on the provincial exam, but great to get your feedback.

NAZ walks through the hallways of PMSS.

NAZ: Senior year at PMSS. Before I could have had a pet iguana, named it Fluffy, and walked it on a leash of banana peels, and still no one would see me. But *Paradise Lost.* Lucky drives his red Mini Cooper straight into Top Lot parking. I move past him and Buddy Cain in front of the rainbow-coloured lockers PMSS painted to make the ethnics feel welcome. I brush Lucky's hand with his Keg mint in my hand . . . the heat from his hand makes a knot. A knot that's one end me, one end Lucky.

NAZ pulls both ends of the Keg mint wrapper like a bow.

A knot so tight no one can loosen it.

LUCKY appears across from NAZ in the hallway in front of the rainbow-coloured lockers.

LUCKY: Everyone! She just stole my lucky Keg mint that I've had ever since the first time I *went* to the Keg! Lucky Punjabi just got violated on by Naznin! And don't try and deny it. You girls are like natural-born liars. Like wearing makeup? And those La Senza bras that make your boobs bigger . . . LIES! Watch out for Naznin! She's a witch who belly-dances for men. Just look at her Egypt necklace!

NAZ: I dance *Indian* classical, and hello?

She holds out her Allah necklace.

Muslim? I'm Ismaili—

LUCKY: No, you're not! You're not "smiley" at all! You're all "frowny" and droopy—

NAZ: *IS*-maili. It's a branch of Islam—

LUCKY: I don't think so. Like I watch Fox News—like, A LOT—and they're always showin' your lot talking in "Egypt"—

NAZ: What about you, Lucky . . . PUNJABI? Shouldn't you be marrying your eight-year-old cousin right now? Oh, I guess hanging out in Surrey and gang-shooting people as they come out of the SkyTrain station keeps you pretty busy, huh?

(to wedding guest) And then it happens. The "cools" laugh. Not at me. For me. Even Buddy and Candice, they all clap and cheer for me. Lucky comes up to me all grown-uppy and pinches my cheek and smiles.

From then on, kids started to *see* me. I was the girl Lucky liked. So I started to look down a lot. Not in an "Indian woman" way, just in a "staying out of the way" WAY. Lucky writes this note saying we should go out, just him and me, Friday night.

> *Flashback: LUCKY and NAZ sit in his Mini Cooper. Chris Brown's "Kiss Kiss" plays from the car stereo.*

LUCKY: I hope you don't mind. I listen to just, like, one song over and over again. I'm weird like that.

NAZ: Lucky buys us a box of doughnuts for dinner and we listen to Chris Brown's "Kiss Kiss" on repeat while we drive out of Port Moody in Lucky's red Mini Cooper, past the yellow sulfur on the

Barnet Highway, over the bridge, and park in front of this West Van mansion.

LUCKY points to the house outside the windshield.

LUCKY: This house has, like, the biggest telly! We can watch through the living-room window! Like a drive-in, yeah?

NAZ: We watch the Friday lineup through Lucky's windshield; no talking, no sound, except for Chris Brown's "Kiss Kiss." I see him looking at me from the corner of my eye. And can see him thinking, "Whoa, her eyelashes are so long." And then he says:

LUCKY: *(staring at NAZ)* You have, like, the longest eyelashes!

NAZ: And nothing feels better than someone thinking you have long eyelashes. Then he hugs me. The CW Network never prepared me for . . . hugging. I let him because there's something in Lucky's arms . . . but then Lucky turns back to the TV.

LUCKY: Miley Cyrus is lickin' a hammer! Oh! When she does it, it's "art." When I do it, it's, "Oh, Lucky Punjabi's drunk!" and "Lucky Punjabi, get out of this Canadian Tire!"

NAZ: I kiss Lucky. And from then on it was every Friday night. Lucky and Naz. I stopped dancing. And wearing my Allah pendant.

NAZ takes off her Allah necklace.

Rehearsal never started on time, and . . . people looking at you all the time . . . After school, we'd all hang out in Top Lot next to Buddy's Hummer, which always took up two parking spots. After Buddy and Candice left, it was finally just me and Lucky driving past the yellow sulphur on the Barnet, going anywhere but here. Listening to songs on repeat—

Present: From the PMSS parking lot, NAZ hears Destiny's Child's "Survivor" blare from the gym.

Is that "Survivor"? I'M JUST GOING TO KILL MYSELF! Fuckin' Port Moody! I HATE YOU SO HARD! Of course those PMSS *assholes* would play "Survivor" for their wedding. Fuckers! PoMo fuckers! This town's such a joke! Wait. You're going in? Why? You *like* this song? *Really*? No, I should stay out here, for Gustakhi. Are the bride and groom in the gym? No, I just really hate that song.

Beat.

Flashback: Early March 2013. NAZ slowly walks into the PMSS gym for a student assembly.

Just before spring break.

We're at one of those dorky school assemblies PMSS holds to give the teachers a break from doing their jobs. I wore a skirt that day, for Lucky.

NAZ appears in a skirt that sits halfway up her thigh.

But I forgot Lucky was driving "the Cooper" to Calgary to audition for *Bhangra Idol*. We all file into the gym and Buddy's sitting by himself in the top bleachers. He fake yawns and pats for me to sit next to him, as a joke. Chris Brown's "Kiss Kiss" is playing on repeat in my head when:

NAZ sits next to BUDDY in the bleachers while tugging down on the hem of her short skirt.

BUDDY: So you got into UBC, huh? That early acceptance bullshit or whatever? Guess you're leaving Port Moody, then? That's mean . . . Leavin' us behind? You're mean. Huh, you cold, meanie? Maybe if you weren't so mean, I'd share my jacket with you. Whoa, your legs look like a gazelle's. My dad and me hunt deer, so I know. Remember when we were at Golden Spike together? I even told Candice, "That Indian chick dancing, she looks like a gazelle."

NAZ: *WE* weren't at Golden Spike together. *LUCKY* and me were performing at Golden Spike.

BUDDY: Lucky? Lucky who?

> *Destiny's Child's "Survivor" plays, starting MEENA and CANDICE's dance performance.*

NAZ: Buddy moves his jacket over both our knees when we start watching Candice and friends dancing to this, like, out-of-nowhere Indian dance by the girls' gym class—

> *Flash to MEENA performing her "Survivor" dance.*

I'm focusing on Meena, the one Indian girl who actually looks like she knows what she's doing, when Buddy grabs my hand under the jacket . . . and moves it . . . on him . . .

> *NAZ's right hand grabs her left wrist, the dance gesture from the Fisherperson Story that describes the fish's words, "I not be happy if I was desired . . ." NAZ remains frozen in this wrist-lock dance gesture.*

. . . on his . . . private . . . on his body? Do you . . . understand what's happening? Because I don't. I don't . . . understand. I keep watching the school-assembly dance while trying to pull my hand back, but Buddy squeezes it there and rolls it in waves, which makes the jacket move. And it's damp— Every time I go over it in my head, I always ask myself, "Why didn't you use your free hand to pull the other hand away?!" That would be a practical application of Indian dance training! One quick— I keep watching the school-assembly dance. I laser-focus on Candice because there's something in my hand that belongs to her. But watching Candice Indian dance, I feel angry because there's something in her hand that belongs to me. Why couldn't that be me down there?

I wish my name was Candice right now and I was down there and she was up here— Why didn't I fight harder? Why didn't my face . . . my face looked like nothing! Like I was just watching this school-assembly dance like it was nothing! Like nothing was happening!

The "Survivor"
dance ends and thunderous
applause rises from the gym bleachers.

The dance ends and Buddy throws away my hand—

NAZ's right hand throws away her left hand, releasing the wrist lock, and her hands transition into clapping along with the rest of the audience in the bleachers.

—and stands up clapping. And I'm just sitting there. I just sit there while Buddy whispers in Candice's ear. He spins her around by her waist and kisses her and calls her his bitch—

NAZ clasps her hands and stops clapping.

I'm so stupid! Stupid for just sitting there, stupid for wearing this skirt, stupid for thinking I was one of "them" because my boyfriend was! Stupid for sitting with Buddy, stupid for not using my hand, for not . . . STUPID for just— Where was Lucky? Why did he have to leave that day? Why would he leave me there alone with Buddy?! Why would he— When I needed him the most . . . WHERE WAS LUCKY?!

Flashback: Akon's "Chammak Challo" plays. LUCKY appears centre stage in a high-school gym for the Bhangra Idol *auditions in Calgary.*

LUCKY: Hello, *Bhangra Idol*! This is *Lucky Punjabi* from Port Moody, BC. And THIS? Is for YOU, Calgary! . . .

LUCKY lip-synchs and dances with full gusto, but is still mediocre at best. His high-energy, bouncing dance moves reach their peak and his audition ends.

Lucky Punjabi OUT!

LUCKY swaggers out and the Akon vocals transitions into the Hamsika Iyer vocal section of "Chammak Challo." NAZ stands alone in an empty high-school gym. She steps into the centre spot where LUCKY was.

NAZ: Lucky was in a gym somewhere, and so was I—

She replicates some of the moves from "Survivor" in time to "Chammak Challo." The dance is a true homage to the Mughal courtesan tradition, with seductive floorwork and the glittering fabric of her encircling skirt. NAZ eventually dances to her feet and at the end she thinks she sees LUCKY and turns in a circle with him. LUCKY exits away from her. NAZ watches him leave. The music has ended and NAZ returns to the PMSS gym.

After the school assembly.

Buddy's hanging all over Candice and looks at me like, "I don't know what you're talking about." Then it starts. At first it was "Naz-ty plus Buddy" in sharp pencil hearts all over the boys' change-room door. Then pictures of me with words next to them.

Without ever looking at it, NAZ opens a locker door that has the words "Would you FUCK this CUNT" written in red paint and a hand-drawn penis below it.

Lucky gets back in time for the test in Mr. Peter Nicholas Smyth's class, and I'm trying to answer "Name that Quote": "I am too far away from you now, talking to you from a land you can't get into with your quick tongue and your hollow heart . . . "—*Antigone*— when the "cools" at the back rub out lit cigarettes into my neck and

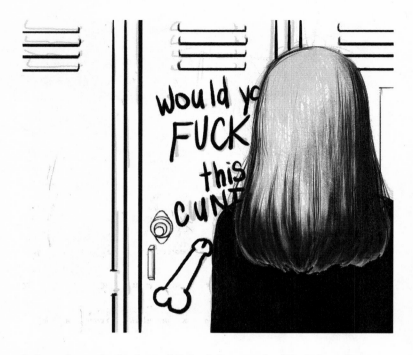

hair and cough, "Ashtray." I don't know why "Penis" can't see, or SMELL, but I keep writing. "I am too far away from you now . . . " And Candice. Candice Paskis corners me in front of the lockers PMSS painted to make the ethnics feel welcome?

CANDICE appears in the company of her girlfriends and corners NAZ against the lockers.

CANDICE: Are you retarded? You weren't even good enough for Lucky; you thought you'd be good enough for Buddy? When Lucky first started talking about you, I was all like, "Who is that? I don't even know who that is." But that you made a move on MY BOYFRIEND? That you thought Buddy'd want to eat out mud when he could lick a snow cone? Before me and Buddy, I offered to go down on Lucky . . . like a couple of times? And he said no 'cause he's hard-core *noble*. But you just look like a bitch. You have a face that looks like a bitch. So shut it off . . . Nazu . . . Nazi—what's your—what's her— *(aside to her friend)* WHAT'S HER NAME, AGAIN?

CANDICE vanishes. NAZ is alone in the hallway.

NAZ: We start volleyball in Miss Flemming's class and there's Emily Johnson, who I was in ensemble dance with just before Christmas break. We danced to "Beep"? The Pussycat Dolls's "Beep"? I showed Emily how to dance a deer with her hand.

NAZ demonstrates the bharatanatyam hand gesture for deer, "Simhamukha."

But Emily's tight with Candice Paskis and throws a volleyball at my head now, but says "oops." Miss Flemming pretends not to see. I say "bitch" softly because it makes me not cry. Miranda Parks smears up against me, "Did you just call Emily a bitch? That's not very nice to say about my *best friend*." And I say, "Well she is. She's a bitch." Emily thuds another volleyball at my face. Harder. After school, Candice's Top Lot friends chase me with lighters and I run. You're not supposed to run in the halls! I don't know why anyone isn't coming out and saying, "Hey! You're not supposed to run in the halls!" I love my eyelashes. They're awesome. They're thick and long and great. My eyelashes are . . . they're really great. Emily thwacks me into a door and my eyelashes get two of my teeth stuck in them. And blood. And bits of door. But it's a red door, so at least it matches.

Adults are always talking about bullying because of annoying girls who cry about being shit-talked on Facebook. But I never said anything because I'm cool like that! Principal Shaker was NOT cool like that. After they take me to the ER to put back my teeth and cauterize my nose bleed, Principal Shaker brings ME into his office for the fifteenth time that month, and along with Penis and Miss Flemming, Principal Shaker tells me I've been become a "distraction" to the other kids, and with provincials coming up, they decide it'd be best for the school if I finished the rest of my year at home, which super-thrills my parents. After school ended, my parents sold our house on Heritage Mountain and left for Dubai. They couldn't look at me anymore. Everything in Port Moody reminded them of me.

There were only another four weeks left till provincial exams started! Eight weeks till graduation! No one gave me a chance to tough it out! *Mother Courage* it out! I could have "silent screamed" my way to graduation, kept my home, my family, my savings, and then I'd be at UBC right now! But instead I'm stuck in this fuckin' Greek tragedy called Port Moody: " . . . talking to you from a land you can't get into with your quick tongue and your hollow heart . . . "

*Flashback: One week before the Victoria Day weekend, 2014.
GUSTAKHI, in her living room, approaches NAZ.*

GUSTAKHI: What happened to Lucky Punjabi? Did Calgary stampede our Lucky out of town? You never told me that part of the story, Naznin. I'm only asking because Lucky phoned me. Lucky's getting married and wants you to dance.

NAZ: LUCKY . . . WHAT? LUCKY . . . WHAT?!

GUSTAKHI: When Lucky left, what song was playing? Which song do you think our Lucky would appreciate—OH GOD! Look at your face, Naznin! *Waah, isey kehte hain ishq.** Relax, *yaar*. Lucky didn't call.

NAZ: ARE YOU KIDDING ME?!

GUSTAKHI: No, it was Buddy. Buddy phoned to ask you to dance for his and this Candice Pakeezah's wedding at your old high school, but the Lucky part I made up. You should use that shock face for dancing; we'd get more tips—

NAZ: You act like me knowing Lucky means *you* knowing Lucky. You *don't* know Lucky! As if I'm going to be all like, "Oh Gustakhi-*jaan*, can we make s'mores and talk about my feelings?" We're not friends like that, so why can't you stop talking about Lucky and just shut up about Lucky?!

GUSTAKHI: BECAUSE I WANT IT TO HURT! STOP AND FEEL IT HURT, Naznin! I've seen you walking around here for the last year, "Oh, I didn't do nothing and see what they all did." But remember: who didn't just pull her hand off his crotch? Who forgot she's a grown girl? A girl who forgot herself; you don't forget that.

NAZ: Then don't you forget to go get yourself laid so you can finally stop masturbating to me and Lucky.

GUSTAKHI: My daughter had a toilet-brush mouth like you too. All modern-thinking, small, thin, look like you can't do, but see what y'all do? My son's engagement day. My daughter gallivants in announcing, informing me in front of everyone, that she too

---

* Translation: This is what they call love?

will be getting married . . . to some low-class boot-polish boy she met at college. Bride's family cancels marriage with my son. Good dowry that we needed? Gone. Then village stops talking to us. Any chance anyone wanted to marry into my family? Do business with my family? Gone. We needed a clean slate. So I told my son, "You take your late daddy's gun, and take your sister into the field."

The Jagjit Singh ghazal "Unke Dekhe Se" plays in the distance.

That morning . . . that old Jagjit Singh ghazal was playing over and over from my neighbour's place when they brought *two* bodies to the village yard . . . Saying it was both murder and suicide? My son too soft and my daughter too loose. The ghazal keeps playing and their bodies just lie there. My blood in dirt. You know what it is to see your own blood lying in dirt? How it is to have the blood in your veins ache and scream at same time? *The cry of the gazelle when it's cornered by the hunter and knows it will die?* My village wouldn't even give them last rites! So *I* built the pyres and watched my children burn. I gave my blood back to Him so their ashes could feed the earth and vegetables. But how could I watch my village eat my family's skin and eyes? So what? Before summer, I was gone.

NAZ: You . . . killed your children? You murdered your . . .

You killed your own blood! And you think you did the RIGHT thing? Was God sitting in your lap saying, "Hey, Gustakhi, do God a solid and kill your daughter for me?!"

GUSTAKHI: Don't YOU talk about God! Don't YOU talk about God like you're chummy-chummy! You know, if you lived anywhere other than here you'd be dead by now. Oh, so sad for "Lucky"? Naznin, you just remember you're the one who's lucky.

NAZ: DON'T SAY HIS NAME! Don't you . . . EVER say his name! EVER! Your awful mouth on his name! Don't talk to me like you and me are somehow the same! Like anything between us is the SAME!

GUSTAKHI: God, you're so Canadian, Naznin. *Haan,* you study classical dance, dance your "Jai Ho!," but you think because you live here you're different than the rest of us when someone takes away everything and you lose *everything*? You know, our ghazal in India isn't just some song the third world made up to kill time. It's the cry of the gazelle when it's cornered by the hunter and knows it will die. So before that happens, I want you to think, Naznin. Eh, Naznin? Are you listening? Naznin?

> *GUSTAKHI snaps her fingers in front of NAZ's face. NAZ jolts as though waking from a deep sleep.*

NAZ: Buddy and Candice are getting married THIS weekend? Lucky's coming back! He wouldn't miss his best friend's wedding! I don't know if I'll feel like dancing for the people who took away everything I ever had . . . THIS weekend.

GUSTAKHI: Did you hear anything I just said—

NAZ: In the Middle East, you cut off a man's hand when he steals something from you? An eye for an eye?

> *NAZ assumes a version of the Natraj statue pose for a moment while maintaining the hand gesture for "one with eyes like a fish" by her eye. Imran Khan's "Amplifier" begins playing in the distance. NAZ places her Allah pendant around her neck again. Present and past tense begin to bleed into each other. NAZ approaches LUCKY's Mini Cooper.*

You tell Buddy and Candice I *will* dance for their wedding. Then you and me will meet at Lucky's Mini Cooper in Bottom Lot just before the reception is supposed to start. You bring out Buddy.

We'll tie him to the car door. And Candice. Candice Paskis. You bring that bitch out here. You bring her and I'll bring all the cigarettes I have. I'll sit in front of Buddy tied to Lucky's red car door and I'll light one and then another and then another, right close to his eyelashes, just to fuck with him. And then when he's good and scared, I'll light a fistful and ASH them in his stupid hand! The cry of the gazelle when it's cornered by the hunter and knows it will die!

GUSTAKHI: Naznin, stop and hear yourself for even a minute—

NAZ: I won't touch Candice! Even though all I want to do is throw her in a pile of sulphur till her bitch face burns off! I'll just make her watch. Even if I have to hold her by her Shoppers Drug Mart–yellow hair and HOOK open her Aryan blue eyes—she's going to SEE ME.

GUSTAKHI: Justice doesn't make living easier, Naznin. I promise it doesn't—

NAZ: I'll keep those cigarettes in that fucker's hand till Buddy's in so much pain he'll do anything for it to stop. And then Buddy'll tell everyone at the PMSS wedding what really happened. Whose hand was *where*, doing *who*, and *what* and *where* and . . . WHAT under that jacket! And then everyone'll know! And Lucky.

> *NAZ lies on the hood of the car.* "Unke Dekhe Se" *faintly plays from the car stereo.*

Lucky will touch my face, and stroke the hair away from my face, and kiss— Buddy and Candice's wedding limousine will be parked in Top Lot, and Lucky'll pick me up in his arms and put me in the limo and we'll just go. And everyone will just watch. We'll sink into the back seat, I'll put my head into that place that fits perfect into Lucky, and we'll *kiss* . . . for all the time we lost . . . for all the time we could have been *kissing*. We'll drive past the sulphur on the Barnet one last time and go.

> *She holds her Allah necklace.*

"I am too far away from you now . . ."

Present: NAZ *is in a half-dream state lying on the hood of* LUCKY'S *car.*

There is no God in Port Moody. So I started wearing this again to call Him back. Even when I sleep. It always somehow swishes over to my left boob, which made me think maybe God was ready to hear my side? That if He could just *hear* my heart, and *feel* my heart, God would stop punishing me and bring back Lucky?

NAZ *suddenly opens her eyes wide, as if waking up from a night-mare. The music is gone.*

ENOUGH! I'm done. I'M DONE. Enough "Jai Ho!" and Top Lots and Bottom Lots and the same song over and over and over and licking the UBC course book like a puppy in a window! How is this fair? Does this seem even a little bit fair, to *you*?! Buddy and Candice are getting married tonight. They're in the gym feeling the happiest they've ever felt . . . And I'm going to take that away!

At long last, GUSTAKHI *arrives in the PMSS parking lot.*

Gustakhi?! Where have you been? I've been waiting all night—

GUSTAKHI: Lucky isn't here. He didn't come for the wedding.

NAZ: You're lying!

GUSTAKHI: Lucky isn't here! Go see with your eyes! Thank God. Now you can cancel this *duffer* plan of yours. What I did was for my family. My name. You want to do this for a boy who gave you a Keg mint?!

She takes LUCKY'S Keg Steakhouse mint from her pocket.

NAZ: It was his LAST Keg mint! From the Keg! Like, you can't just get those! You actually have to eat a full steak dinner at the Keg! And he told me to hold on to it!

She dances the "knot" hand gesture.

We made a knot! You don't just forget that!

GUSTAKHI: You want to right the wrong, punish Buddy and Candice? But what about Lucky? You're not Romeo and Juliet. Where is he? You know what Gustakhi thinks? Gustakhi thinks when Lucky came back from Calgary and everyone believed *you* put your hand on Buddy? He believed it too.

Flashback: Early March 2013, in the evening. LUCKY, freshly returned from auditioning in Calgary, sits in his car with NAZ in the parking lot at PMSS.

LUCKY is in the driver's seat.

LUCKY: Buddy told me everything last night. Candice too. While I was singing in Calgary, you were . . . I can't even look at you, Naznin. Dubee was sitting right behind you and Buddy in the top-row bleachers.

NAZ: You're not even going to let me tell my side?!

Present.

GUSTAKHI: Tell me your side, Naznin! Your side, his side, but tell SOME SIDE! Scream, yell, abuse him, but really look back and remember what—what really happened—

Flashback.

LUCKY: Are you going to tell me that you *didn't* have Buddy's cock in your hand? That the second I left you alone . . .

Beat.

I should have known—the way he looked at you—

NAZ: The way HE looked at ME! Let's just go for a drive. And then we can talk and we can go for a drive—

Present.

GUSTAKHI: What drive? You have to dance now, Naz! But get this out of your system. Burning Buddy's hand won't fix nothing—

NAZ: You know how everyone was super stressed out about Rihanna and Chris Brown and how maybe they hooked up again? But looking from the outside doesn't mean you know! You don't know anything! Even if everyone else says so, you have to hear both sides!

Flashback.

LUCKY: I don't have to hear any sides. I know. I kissed Candice tonight. She's a really good Indian dancer. Better than you. She was telling me how she's going to the Coventry School of Bhangra. And I kissed her, but then I stopped because—

Present.

GUSTAKHI: Where was Lucky when those ugly girls threw volley-balls at your face, Naznin? When Lucky's boy friends ashed their cigarettes in your neck and hair in class—

Flashback.

LUCKY: In Hindi, the word for "trouble"—it's feminine. You're *taqleef*, Naznin. You tricked me into kissing my best friend's girl!

She pulls out the Keg mint.

NAZ: But we made a knot!! You don't make a knot for nothing. A knot makes us family! Lucky?

NAZ reaches out to touch LUCKY.

L U C K Y aggres- sively s w a t s NAZ away.

LUCKY: SLUT, DON'T TOUCH ME!!

NAZ: *(shocked)* LUCKY . . .

Present.

GUSTAKHI: Family isn't just driving around in a car and "*main yahaan, tum wahaan.*"* Family is for when things get tough.

Flashback.

LUCKY: I should have known better! You prostitute-dance for men!

NAZ: I stopped dancing for you!

LUCKY: I have to get away from you!

---

* Translation: "I'm way over here, and you're way over there."

LUCKY gets out of his car. NAZ rushes out behind him to the middle of the parking lot.

NAZ: PLEASE, LUCKY! STOP! YOU HAVE TO STOP! I CAN'T . . . I don't know what . . . YOU HAVE TO STOP . . .

Present.

GUSTAKHI: Things got just a little tough, and Lucky ran? Have some "Naz," Naz! *Some* pride! See what you became with Lucky?

Flashback: LUCKY is outside of his car.

LUCKY: I have to get away from you. I don't think I'll be back for graduation. My car broke down on the way back from Calgary, so I'm just leaving it here in Bottom Lot.

NAZ sinks down to the pavement.

NAZ: Please, Lucky. Please don't do this! Don't punish me! I'M SO STUPID! I wore a skirt that day! At the school assembly? I wore a stupid skirt that day because I forgot you weren't going to be there. I'm so stupid! I sat next to Buddy! I should have known better! When he took my hand—

NAZ's right hand grabs her left wrist, assuming the dance position she took to tell the story of what happened in the bleachers during the school assembly.

I should have fought him harder. I should have tried harder. I should have thought about you! I should have thought about how much

I love you and then I would have fought harder! I'm sorry! I don't know what else to do! I'm so sorry, Lucky . . . PLEASE!

Beat.

Can I at least look after your car for you—

LUCKY: Look after my car?! Look after— You can't even drive, Naznin! And even if you could . . . My car is my God. I'd never trust you with my God.

Present.

GUSTAKHI: You're wearing your Allah necklace again? Keep wearing it, so you know God hasn't forgotten you. I wish He'd remember me. It's been twenty years since . . . my children. And ever since my life has been a constant Ramadan. Going without my whole life. But I'm ready for Eid, Naznin. I'm not even Muslim but I'm ready for Eid. I want my feast and forgiveness.

Flashback.

LUCKY: I have to go . . .

Present.

NAZ: I have to go.

GUSTAKHI: What? You have to dance. Do your job then go back to the house.

NAZ: No, I mean I can't dance for these weddings anymore. I can't look at that sulphur anymore. I was supposed to go to university! How did I get here? How did I get myself here? I have to go . . . now . . .

GUSTAKHI: Don't . . . run like Lucky. Be proud like Naz. Do your job then leave. Go. They're waiting.

Imran Khan's "Amplifier" begins playing as NAZ walks up the steep hill to the PMSS gym lit by the glow of parking lights and street lamps and wet pavement.

NAZ: Here we go. When we get in there, can you maybe stay with me for a bit? Thanks. Yeah, all I have to do is walk up the hill. Past Bottom Lot. Past Middle Lot. Past Top Lot. Funny, from here, doesn't it look like the gym's being surrounded? Like all these boys with cars have her backed in and she has nowhere to run? . . . Cornered by the hunter . . .

> *NAZ enters the PMSS gym where* BUDDY *and* CANDICE's *wedding reception is in full swing. The gym looks like it did for the graduation dance in* Fish Eyes, *minus the Starlight Taj Mahal theme; the lights are dim, the decorations are cheap, and a disco ball turns in the background.*

This is it. The PMSS gym. I see Candice Paskis, who's nine months preggers. And I see Buddy got a stupid haircut . . . that makes him look stupid.

BUDDY steps up on a makeshift riser while holding a glass of sparkling wine to address his wedding-reception audience. He taps the side of his wine glass with a plastic fork.

BUDDY: Some of you all know, because of the baby, my dad took back my Hummer. But it's okay, guys, because me and Candice are taking turns riding my sister's mountain bike— Yeah, Top Lot rules! Candice? Babe? The universe threw us a curve ball, but we will rise again, 'cause nothing's gonna get us down. Not even a broken condom.

NAZ looks at the crowd around her.

NAZ: Look at these PMSSers! Do you see these Top Lot douchebags listening to this like, "Oh my God, that's love!" And they all have stupid haircuts too! It's like these assholes got a Groupon to get stupid haircuts! But I don't see Lucky. And yet I see him so clearly now. And I hear . . . The cry of the gazelle. I should get on stage— Buddy?

BUDDY: Hey! We're all super excited to see you dance. You still look, like . . . like you really stayed in shape and stuff. Too bad Lucky's not here, right? I just wanted to say . . . about last year? I wanted to say sorry . . . for Candice. She said some pretty nasty stuff and then you had to drop out . . .

NAZ: You want to say sorry . . . for Candice?

BUDDY: Yeah, and Emily and them too; they were really out of line. But are we cool?

Beat.

NAZ: Are we cool? You're a bitch, Buddy. You have a face that looks like a bitch.

NAZ looks to the audience.

Let's do this!

Chris Brown's "Kiss Kiss" begins to play and the lights shift to a spotlight on NAZ *at centre stage.* NAZ *unzips her hoodie and takes it off to reveal a sparking sari blouse underneath.* NAZ *jumps off the makeshift stage and the spotlight follows her as she approaches the crowd, who circles around her. She stares at each of them directly in the eyes and then begins moving.* NAZ *dances for* BUDDY *and* CANDICE's *reception with power and distinction because she is dancing for herself. The dance is a true demonstration of* NAZ's *skill because her movements are as precise as they are wild. She plays with Chris Brown's set rhythms, sometimes working with them and sometimes against, but it is clear that she is calling*

*the shots, not the music. Kicks and jumps and footwork are laced
with tight spins that make* NAZ's *skirt glitter in the air, but ultimately the dance ends with simple Kathak footwork directly in
front of the audience as* NAZ *stares each audience member in the
eye. With one last stomp, the song ends and* NAZ *exits the gym
through unanimous, thunderous applause without taking a bow.*

NAZ *walks outside and spots a heavily decorated bike that has a
bright "Just Married" sign on it and some tin cans and stream-
ers trailing off the back.* NAZ *looks at the bike. "Unke Dekhe
Se" starts playing in the distance.* NAZ *takes* LUCKY's *Keg mint
out of her pocket, unwraps it, and pops it into her mouth as she
peacefully looks across the horizon of sulphur. Abruptly,* NAZ *spits
the mint out onto the pavement.*

Ugh! How old is this mint?

NAZ *gets a backpack and slings it over her shoulder.*
NAZ *goes to the bike and rips off the
"Just Married" sign, throwing it
to the ground. She looks down
the length of the Barnet
Highway in front of
her and then walks
the bike urgently
towards it, leaving
Port Moody.*

Blackout.

End of play.

LET ME BORROW THAT TOP

Let Me Borrow That Top was co-commissioned by Nightswimming and The Banff Centre. It was developed and produced by Nightswimming and premiered at the Cultch in Vancouver as part of the PuSh International Performing Arts Festival on January 28, 2015, with the following cast and creative team:

Choreographer and actor: Anita Majumdar
Director and dramaturg: Brian Quirt
Producer: Rupal Shah
Stage manager: Sandy Plunkett
Lighting design: Rebecca Picherack
Set and costume design: Jackie Chau
Projection and sound design: Christopher Stanton
Production manager: Simon Rossiter

Let Me Borrow That Top should never be performed in isolation. The play must always be produced as a companion to *Boys With Cars*, either in a double bill or in the full trilogy.

Characters

Candice
Buddy

The hit Bollywood song "Chikni Chameli" plays in darkness. The lights come up on an empty teenage girl's bedroom. On a desk lay a series of makeup containers and brushes, a mirror, and a laptop. Cardboard moving boxes are piled up behind the desk. An actress of colour enters and sits behind the desk silently and prepares to perform her role as CANDICE. *She shows the audience (the YouTube camera on her laptop) a contact-lens container by laying it flat against her palm. The flat palm resembles the bharatanatyam hand gesture "Pataka." She opens the container and puts a blue contact lens in her right eye and then her left. The actress's eyes are now blue. She then takes out a long, wavy blond wig and strokes it next to her face in front of the laptop camera. She shows off a bobby pin against her palm and begins pinning*

*the wig into her own dark hair. After she's done, the actress
looks proudly at the camera and to her audience. The music fades
out.* CANDICE *addresses her YouTube audience. September 2013.*

CANDICE: *(waves)* Hey, guys! It's me, Candice Paskis! C-Pac. So I
know I haven't made a video all summer. Like how did Labour Day
weekend get here already, right?! I'm reeeeaaaally sorry, you guys.
Summer's been suuuuuuuper busy. I just graduated in June. Some of
you guys know that from my Grad Dance Look Tutorial I did with
my boyfriend, Buddy. And thanks for all your great comments about
me and Buddy! Buddy's great . . . Except we broke up. AT GRAD.
And then we got back together for like . . . a minute . . . LITERALLY.

> CANDICE *takes out a home-pregnancy test that's already
> been used.*

But now we're off for sure. We haven't talked in like . . . since August
long weekend?

> CANDICE *takes out a kitchen timer and twists the dial.*

Time really . . .

> *She dials the timer to thirty minutes.*

. . . HEALS, you know?

And oh my gawd! Two thousand subscribers! Thanks sooooo much,
you guys. I know a lot of you are from Hong Kong and Viet-wan.
And a lot of you who are Hongkanese; you've been asking about
my everyday look. TokyoGirl83 said I looked like Carmindy from
TLC's *What Not to Wear*! You guuuuuuuyyyyyyyys! That's sooooo

sweet. She's super pretty. Carmindy, I mean. Not TokyoGirl83. Sorry.

So for my hair I use L'Oréal Superior Preference Ultra Light Blonde No. 1, but I think for most of you guys who subscribe to me, your hair's too muddy, like there's too much pigment in your hair shaft, so you should just get extensions. But the hard part is your face. I can help you fix that. I'm going to show you my morning routine and I'm always going to tell you what I'm using and what brush I'm using it with.

> CANDICE *focuses on the pregnancy test for a moment while shaking a bottle of foundation. She acknowledges the pregnancy test is a distraction and puts it out of sight.*

So I'm just going to talk for a bit . . . or like, whatev . . . Oh! Sorry! L'Oréal's True Match: Classic Ivory No. 1.

> CANDICE *presents a vertical container of peach colour flat against her palm for the camera. She pours the liquid foundation out onto a stainless-steel plate.*

So a lot of you have been mentioning my positivity in my videos, like just the way I talk?

> CANDICE *dots her face with liquid foundation makeup.*

I'm generally a pretty positive person—Candice Paskis, the "P" is for "Positive." My sister and me started reading the *I Ching* together while we were Christmas shopping last year. It's this Szechuanese self-help book we found in the bargain section of Chapters. It's like the Book of Change? And my sister and me were all like, "Ugh!

I just want it to be different already!" you know? Oh, sorry! I'm talking about my sister Kayla. So not Kelly, who married the railway guy from Sarnia. And not Kaitlin—she's three. And NOT Brittany.

> CANDICE *smears the dotted foundation around her face with a makeup sponge.*

She's the one I told you about who came to Zumba class with me and my best friend Emily Johnson and my best friend Miranda and my best friend Michelle B. and Michelle G. And Brittany was all like Zumba-ing like a *whore.* And that was after Brittany crashed Cody Kochmar's wedding to my *best friend* Dana Allen, who was pregnant. But Brittany shows up in this skank red dress that's not even a dress! It's a red top that's two sizes too small, which is *so* disrespectful to the bride, Dana, who was super fat and didn't even look good . . . 'Cause she was pregnant! Duh! Dana Allen's my best friend; I'd never talk bad about her.

Concealer! So you guys know how much I love-love-loooooooooove my Laura Mercier Camouflage concealer in No. 1.

> CANDICE *snatches a brown square container and displays it against her flat palm for the camera.*

No lie, super pricey. Like this was pretty much my whole paycheque, but it lasts forever. I'm using a flat foundation brush from Quo—

> *She displays the foundation brush against her flat hand for the audience.*

—which you can get at any Shoppers. So maybe try your local China version, "Choppers."

CANDICE applies concealer with a brush under her eyes and over blemishes around her mouth.

So yeah, my sister Kayla and me were reading the *I Ching*, which sounds like an iPhone app, except it's super legit. Super positive. But says it how it is. Like I started stepping up more. And I already do that with babysitting Kaitlin and making dinner and doing the driving when my mom's working or she's out drinking at Roosters. My brother Connor's *supposed* to do the driving, but he's usually getting high with Cody, so . . . and Brittany's just a *whore.*

CANDICE turns towards her bedroom door and shouts through the walls.

BRITTANY! CAN I BORROW THAT RED TOP FROM DANA'S WEDDING?

CANDICE waits to hear an answer through her bedroom wall. Silence.

(back to the audience) WHORE. But I just decided I needed to take charge of my life the way I do for our house. Speaking of—

CANDICE takes out a round container and brush and displays it against her palm for the camera.

I use Rimmel's Sun Bronzer with E.L.F's Contour Brush so I look more cut, and I don't have to work out. But what I find really helps with that is only eating a pack of Skittles for lunch. But guys, I don't want to talk about health and fitness in *this* video. I'll do a separate one for that.

What was I saying? Oh yeah! Change your life!

CANDICE sucks in her cheeks and aggressively colours in the angles of her cheekbones with her brush and bronzer.

So, you guys remember my Starlight Taj Mahal–theme grad? At first I didn't think I could plan a whole grad dance by myself. But then I was like, "What would the *I Ching* do?" So I decided to make the best Indian-theme grad dance ever. *I Ching*, ladies. Book of change. You gotta bull-horn it. Take the bull by the horns. Bull. Horn. *IT*. And by bull-horning it? I ching-chong-CHANGED my life!

Grad Committee was meeting just before Christmas break and booked some lame hotel in Vancouver that had NO theme, so me and Buddy went to go buy bindis and mangoes, to show the grad committee I meant business. I really worked on my Starlight Taj Mahal Grad presentation. And PENIS—Mr. Peter Nicholas Smyth—said it was the best presentation he'd ever seen in his life. For sure, Starlight Taj Mahal Grad 2013? Was the beginning of everything good.

But change can't happen if you don't love yourself. Like if you don't *love* yourself, you need to SHUT UP because you're never going to fight for yourself if you think you don't deserve it. Which is why I broke up with Buddy this summer.

Before I forget, I need to set this!

She points to her face.

CANDICE pulls out a round container and presents it flat against her palm for the camera.

I use CoverGirl's Loose Powder in Light, but the puff they give with it is crap! That's why I use my own powder puff.

CANDICE takes a round velour puff and rubs it against her skin while speaking in a baby voice.

I looooove my puff so much!

CANDICE starts patting her face down with so much powder she looks like a chalkboard chamois.

This year wasn't *all* good though. Like even though I was nailing organizing Starlight Taj Mahal Grad, and I felt super smart and stuff, just before spring break was a really hard time. Like intersocialally? It was right around the time I was doing everything around the house and my mom was trolling Roosters like aaaaaaaall the time, and Kaitlin kept drawing on the walls and Brittany wouldn't even help me clean it off.

CANDICE turns towards her bedroom door again and shouts to her sister.

BRITTANY! LET ME BORROW THAT TOP FROM DANA'S WEDDING!

CANDICE waits to hear an answer through her bedroom wall. Silence.

(to audience) BITCH. I can't remember if I told you guys about my ex-boyfriend, Shane? He was the one who couldn't shut his mouth off about how I offered to go down on Buddy at Golden Spike Fest. Uh, I offered to go down on *Lucky*, not Buddy, dipshit! You guys remember Lucky Punjabi, right? He's this wicked Indian singer from my school.

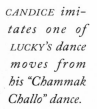

CANDICE imitates one of LUCKY'S dance moves from his "Chammak Challo" dance.

So we're all at Golden Spike Fest, which is like our Port Moody fourth of July, only on July first. And I'm wearing my red-sequin bra from La Senza and my Stampede cowboy hat to show everyone I was *serious* about summer. But Buddy and his boys were all watching stupid Naz and her stupid, slow Indian dance. Even Lucky . . . Phht, I could do that . . . Lucky . . . But the night of Golden Spike—after all the performances—me and Lucky have, like, the *best* conversation . . . after he said "no" to going down on him. We just talked forever. We talked about England—where he's from—then he told me he had a thing for this Indian girl. But then! He gives me . . . his lucky Keg mint! And he tells me to hold onto it for him. Because that's how good friends we are now.

So then I found Buddy and we did stuff till Shane caught us. So senior year at PMSS, Shane gets his revenge. *Shane* goes and finds my *mom* at Roosters one night and they hook up! So I'm sitting there having breakfast Monday morning with my mom and *Shane*. And then I had to go Indian dance for this school assembly THAT DAY? But I bull-horned it. I slapped a bindi on my face and I kicked that school-assembly dance in the BALLS.

CANDICE holds a rectangular container of blush flat against her palm for the camera.

You want to apply blush to the *balls* of your cheeks—but just pinch your cheeks. Save the money and break some blood vessels . . .

CANDICE smiles wider in order to grab more skin.

. . . But not so much you look like you got slapped.

Oh my gawd . . . So, some people think Lucky liked me . . .

She plays with her hair.

Or whatever? I mean no one ever came out and said it, but I know they were thinking it. I think it's because I was always laughing whenever he was around, and he never touched me, even though I touched him, like, all the time . . . as a joke! But then I walked in on him and Naz kissing and . . . it made my heart hurt a little bit.

CANDICE takes out an eyeliner pen and presents it flat against her palm for the camera.

So, I like doing a Rihanna-meets-*Teen Mom* eye. I start with L'Oréal's Lineur Intense because it's really black. But not TOO much because it's daytime?

CANDICE applies way too much eyeliner while speaking and flicks the liner up to look like fish tails. She speaks while intricately applying her eyeliner.

Naz never even appreciated him. Bitch. Like I hate when people use that word . . . except when I use it about *other* people. But she is! "Oh, I'm Naz and I got into *UBC*! Oh, I'm Naz, and I Indian dance like a gazelle. Oh I'm Naz! And I CONSPIRACY-ED Lucky to go to Calgary!" So then he couldn't see *Candice* dance like a gazelle! I bet she never even read the *I Ching*. Racist. Like, harsh prejudice, for sure.

But I kind of had an ace up my sleeve with my school-assembly dance. Like if Lucky could've just seen me Indian dance, I could have stopped him from getting his heart hurt.

But Lucky was singing in Calgary that day, which I'm pretty sure was thanks to Naz.

But as soon as Lucky got back, he came straight to *my* house. God like, for sure, works in mysterious ways. Lucky brings over this Indian movie called *Kiss-me*. Like my name: Candice Pas-*KIS*. It's like the most roman-tical movie in Indian history. There's this white girl who's like the prettiest in the whole movie. And she and this Indian guy, they can't be together.

On her iPod CANDICE *plays the theme song from Kisna, "Hum Hain Is Pal Yahan," which underscores the scene.*

So we're watching and then Lucky? Frenches me! Out of the blue . . . after I Frenched him first. He was saying I should totally apply to the Coventry School of Bhangra in the UK. Then he started teaching me his moves in my basement . . .

CANDICE *dances* LUCKY'S *Bhangra moves in her chair.*

That's when I Frenched him. But then he stopped 'cause he said he couldn't do that to Naz. So then he went to go kiss *her* and do stuff . . . with *her.*

CANDICE *turns off her iPod.*

Flashback: CANDICE *arrives with her gang of girlfriends to corner* NAZ *in the hallway of rainbow-coloured lockers in her version of the scene.*

Are you retarded? You weren't good enough for Lucky; you thought you'd be good enough for Buddy? That you thought Lucky . . . BUDDY! That you thought BUDDY'D want to eat out mud when he could lick a snow cone? When Lucky first started talking about you, I was all like, "Who is that? I don't even know who that is!" But you just look like a bitch. You have a face that looks like a bitch. So shut it off . . . Nazu . . . Nazi—what's your, what's her— *(aside to someone)* WHAT'S HER NAME, AGAIN?

Present: In her bedroom with her YouTube audience. Beat.

I knew her name.

But it didn't matter because Lucky already booked it out of Port Moody . . . MASCARA!

*CANDICE takes out a tube of mascara and aggressively pumps
the mascara wand in and out.*

I'm using my favourite, Buxom's Amplified. Again, super expensive, but not if you steal the tester from Sephora. Fact? It's not stealing if you steal the tester. Like they're not allowed to arrest you because testers have no cash value, which means it's free. At least in Canada. I don't know how it is in less good countries, but I know it's the rule here because I used to work at Shoppers . . . before they fired me for stealing all the testers. But they didn't *arrest* me because they weren't allowed.

*"Chammak Challo" begins to underscore from CANDICE's iPod.
CANDICE opens the tube of mascara.*

Seriously, I love this mascara. I got on a ten-hour plane ride to England with this on?

*CANDICE nonchalantly zigzags the mascara wand from the roots
to her upper lashes quickly.*

And it was still totally perfect and spidery when I landed. Girls of the world, beware. Candice Paskis . . . the official Black Widow!

Flashback: England.

CANDICE flings off her dressing robe to reveal a blue salwar kameez. Her bedroom desk transforms into an antique desk and her backdrop turns into a stuffy English office. CANDICE is now at her interview for the Coventry School of Bhangra in England. Victoria Day weekend, May 2013.

(respectfully) Thanks so much, Mr. Sharma.

Happy Victoria Day long weekend! I know you said my video audition was good enough for my Coventry School of Bhangra application, but I'm graduating in June—oh my God, next month! And I don't really know what I'm doing after, so I just decided to come to England and have you see me. Live.

Right. So we were doing this dance component in gym class? And we all had to come up with an ensemble dance number, and the best group in the class got to perform in a school-assembly dance in front of the entire school. And my group got picked! Everyone was really impressed, including this Indian girl in our group, *Teena*?

She showed us how to do these—

> CANDICE *sloppily demonstrates the spins that* MEENA *initially suggested for the "Survivor" dance.*

—which I didn't know Indian dance even *did* spins! I suggested we do that at the end of the dance. And that's how I made the dance. Look. I super know I'm not Indian, and I'm not trying to be offensive or whatever. It just doesn't seem fair, Mr. Sharma. I want this from my *heart*, but if Indian people are all like, "Oh, that's *my* stuff. Don't touch my stuff. That's mine . . . Ahh!" when most of them don't even eat samosas anymore, that's weird to me. Like . . . *my* aunt. She can't have kids because she got an abortion when she was sixteen and it ruined her junk. So when she moved to BC, my sister Brittany was just born, and my aunt saw Brittany as the dead fetus she never had. So fifteen years later my aunt buys Brittany this super cute red top . . . from Metrotown—and it wasn't even her birthday! My aunt just buys it for Brittany because she thinks she's special, but Brittany hardly ever wears it! So I ask if I can wear it because that's what I'd do with a top like that. I'd wear it. I'd wear it real good. But Brittany's all like, "No. It's *my* top and I get to do what I want with it because it's mine." And it just makes me feel like . . . like . . . LET ME BORROW THAT TOP, BRITTANY! YOU'RE NOT EVEN WEARING IT?! I just think I deserve that top. 'Cause that day at the school assembly? After everything that happened at the *school assembly*? The least I deserve is that red top.

   Beat.

Just before spring break.

I was dancing, but I was looking for Lucky, Buddy's best friend, Lucky Punjabi? I was so sure he'd be there. But he wasn't. He was singing in Calgary that day. Oh, Buddy's my boyfriend.

Would I miss Buddy if I went to school here? Um . . . no. And I'm not just saying that because I really want to go here. He kind of cheated on me during my school-assembly dance.

Flashback: Early March 2013. CANDICE *dances her inexperienced version of the floorwork section of "Survivor" while speaking.*

While I was dancing for the whole school . . . next to Teena—

   MEENA *suddenly appears on her feet doing a slower spinning section of the "Survivor" dance. Her grace and many years of honed skill become even more evident in comparison to* CANDICE.

CANDICE takes MEENA's place and MEENA disappears. CANDICE walks to the bleachers to where BUDDY and NAZ are sitting.

Buddy was in the bleachers with this Indian girl—Naz—and they were . . .

NAZ's right hand grabs her left wrist in the same wrist-lock gesture she made at the school assembly when BUDDY made his move on her. CANDICE reappears.

. . . WHILE I was dancing!

CANDICE performs the rest of "Survivor," but the distraction of her rage keeps her a little behind the beat of the song. After the spinning section, CANDICE has to take a moment to catch her breath, but joins the dance again to hit the final gesture while staring down BUDDY in the bleachers.

Positive people don't swear, right? But Buddy's always like, "<*beep, beep, beep*>! Yeah, dog, she's my <*beep-beep beep*>, and I'm gonna <*beep-beep*> her after I <*beep-beep*> her!" And I'm just standing there surviving. Barely.

Why am I with Buddy? Because Shane broke up with me. And before him, it was Shane's brother, Dom, Dubee . . . Brent Brown . . . Jef with one F . . . Yeah, ever since grade seven I've always had a boyfriend. But dancing that school-assembly dance was the first time I was okay not being next to a guy, 'cause I felt like I was swimming? Or, like, free, or whatever.

Buddy's hanging all over me after my school-assembly dance that I poured everything into and I'm talking to the Indian girl, Teena, but then Buddy whispers in my ear:

BUDDY: Ditch the Paki and meet me in Top Lot. I don't know why. I feel like "smushin.'"

Back in Mr. Sharma's office.

CANDICE: I can't breathe! He spins me around by my waist and kisses me? And calls me his? I can't breath. Sorry, I really can't—

She gasps for air.

I can't brea— Can I have that water, Mr. Sharma? Because I can't—I can't—I CAN'T BREATHE!

CANDICE takes a glass of water and gulps it all down. She tries to get her breath back. Beat.

I can't help thinking maybe there's something better? Like maybe I could *do* better? *That's* why I came to England, Mr. Sharma. Better, to me, means going to the Coventry School of Bhangra.

Present: CANDICE *is at her bedroom desk filming her YouTube video.*

Fan mail time! This one's FolkloreFromLahore from Pakistan, who asks how I get my eyebrows to NOT match my hair. Where's my pencil . . . Ugh! Sorry, guys, everything's in boxes right now. Packing for school. Super annoying . . . but exciting, right?!

CANDICE *grabs an eye pencil off the edge of her desk.*

So I'm filling my brows with this brown Wet n Wild pencil, which is the same colour as my real hair, so it's kind of like I'm paying tribute to my roots . . . Huh! Get it?

CANDICE *draws on her eyebrows so she looks like a Muppet.*

I hope you guys are bookmarking this video because I probably won't be able to make as many videos from England. Oh! Did I even tell you guys? Duh! I start at the Coventry School of Bhangra in two weeks! For those of you who don't know, Bhangra is this super ancient, super hard Indian dance from India-England. I found out I got in just before my Starlight Taj Mahal Grad Dance—

CANDICE *begins applying red lipstick.*

And everyone was wearing something Indian! Like a bindi! And a henna tattoo. But then Buddy pulls me up to Top Lot parking and he's all like, "So what? You wanna <*beep-beep-beep*> marry me or <*beep-beep-beep*> what, bitch?"

CANDICE *gets up from her chair. Remembering her audience, she points to her very red lips.*

Oh. I'm wearing Rimmel's Jet Set Red.

Flashback: CANDICE *is in the PMSS parking lot next to the gym with* BUDDY *on grad night, June 2013.*

(to BUDDY*)* Are you retarded? This is supposed to be the most *Twilight*-ical moment of my life!

CANDICE *holds a bindi on the tip of her middle finger.*

Are you for real giving me an engagement BINDI?! The FREE bindi everyone got at the door when they showed up to grad? The grad *I* organized?! So basically I just bought my own *engagement bindi*?!

BUDDY: Whoa, babe, the bride isn't supposed to yell at the guy when he proposes. Stop being a cunt and just wear your fuckin' bindi—

CANDICE: Gaaaaw-duh! STOP SWEARING at me! Stop trying to hold me . . . with your . . . hands!

BUDDY: Babe, are you saying no to my engagement bindi? Why are you saying all this stuff—

CANDICE: BECAUSE I WANT YOU TO HURT! God, that you would touch me with that hand! What kind of manwhore pulls a girl's hand onto his own crotch in public! While *I* was dancing right in front of you! And then you're all jacked up from Naz's hand job and you want me to go up with you to Top Lot to finish you off?! And then we get to your car and what do I see in the back seat? *BRITTANY'S RED TOP?! That's* how we celebrated my first Indian dance show?! When you first told me about Naz I never said, "Buddy! That doesn't make sense. Naz harsh loves Lucky." Why didn't I say that? Why did I believe you?

"Survivor" starts to play faintly from the gym.

So I'm dancing fuckin' "Survivor" and you're fuckin' rubbing one out with her hand on your fuckin' . . . And then you fuck *me* on top of my cunt sister's RED TOP?! You spun me around my waist, and kissed me, and you called me *your* bitch like nothing happened!

"Survivor" ends.

If you were going to make a move on a girl, it should have been with someone you would've actually broken up with me for. Like Lucky? If I thought Lucky liked me even a little bit? For real, I would have left Port Moody with him. FOR SURE. And nothing could have stopped me. You could have pulled me by my hair and you still couldn't have stopped me. I would've just taken some scissors and cut my hair off with your hands still in it, and I LOVE my hair, but nothing would've stopped me from going.

I applied to this Indian dance school and I got in. I'm going to England, Buddy. I'm *not* marrying you. I'm going, and that's that.

BUDDY: Lucky? My best . . . Lucky? But . . . but you don't even know anything about Indian dance . . .

CANDICE: Yeah I do! Remember the *(searching)* . . . "Fish Eyes" dance I choreographed for the school!

BUDDY: *(trying not to cry)* But you're my bitch? You can't go do Indian dance!

CANDICE: Are you crying?

She rolls her eyes and lets out a loud sigh.

Look, I'm sorry your feelings are hurt, but I'm going to England. And I'm going to the Coventry School of Bhangra. And I'm sorry you're obviously way more into me? Than I'm into you!

Present: CANDICE *sits back down at her makeup desk and addresses her YouTube audience.*

And THAT's? How you do your *makeup*!

CANDICE *looks towards the door and yells.*

BRITTANY! I'M TAKING THAT TOP!

Back to her YouTube audience.

Girls like Brittany are always taking stuff! But I'm not gonna let that get me down because I'm going to England. I'm going to become the greatest Indian dancer ever! And I'm going to find Lucky and he's going to KISS ME . . . And no one's taking that away. Not Brittany with her red dress that's just a top. Not Naz with her UBC and, "Oh, I'm an Indian dance deer!"

CANDICE tries to do the bharatanatyam gesture for deer—"Sim-hamukha"—with her hand but can't and gives up.

And NOT that fish-eyes chick with all her spins who never got dizzy once. Look at my makeup! Ivory No. 1, Laura Mercier No. 1, Superior Preference No. 1! Because positive people who don't swear always come up NUMBER ONE!

CANDICE is interrupted by the kitchen timer bell. CANDICE turns to look at her pregnancy test.

FUCK.

Snap black out. The Pussycat Dolls's "Beep" plays. Lights

up. *The actress of colour playing* CANDICE *(no longer in her blond wig) dances a version* KALYANI AUNTY'*s gestures from the Fisherperson Story from* Fish Eyes *and* NAZ'*s "Amplifier" and "Kiss Kiss" dances from* Boys With Cars. *The actress of colour mischievously plays with the gender roles of the voices, singing "Beep" while injecting a polished refinement into the Fisherperson Story dance moves. The actress of colour ends by landing the Natraj statue position with the gesture for "one with eyes like a fish." The last sound is the censored "beep" at the end of the song.*

Lights to black.

End of play.

ACKNOWLEDGEMENTS

After eleven years, I am indebted to a village of people: Layne Coleman, Brian Quirt, Rupal Shah, Sandy Plunkett, Sherry Bie, Blair Francey, Philip Akin, Rebecca Picherack, Jackie Chau, Chris Stanton, Mark Cassidy, Nina Okens, Stephanie Nakamura, David Yee, Casey Prescott, Carolyn Warren, Nightswimming Theatre, Emma Mackenzie Hillier, Rachel Steinberg, Leora Morris, Sue Edworthy, Paula Forst, Joseph Pierre, Dian Marie Bridge, Karim Morgan, Djennie Laguerre, David Collins, Marie Fewer-Muncic, Guillermo Verdecchia, Elaine Lumley, Sal Bertoli, Abhishek Mathur, Jyoti Rana, Raakhi Sinha Kapur, Gurpreet Sian, Marcus Youssef, Ellie O'Day, South Asian Arts, NeWorld Theatre, Norman Armour, the PuSh Festival, Asha Vijayasingham, Molly McGlynn, Ranvir Shah, Hari Krishnan, Eric Coates, Andy Cheng, Richie Mehta, Aengus Finnan, Chris Abraham, Tina Rasmussen, Allison Bottomley, Franco Boni, Summerworks Festival, the National Theatre School of Canada, the Canada Council for the Arts, the Ontario Council for the Arts, John Murrell, Kelly Robinson, Yvette Nolan, Donna-Michelle St. Bernard, Tamara Dawit, Sheniz Janmohamed, Kate Schlemmer, Maryth Yachnin, Mark Williams, Charlotte Corbeil-Coleman, and my dear partner in life, Nicco Lorenzo Garcia.

To the National Theatre School of Canada 2004 Acting Class—
Gemma, Andrew, Hernan, Marc, Shelley, Dalal, Peter, Trent,
Gregory—thank you for teaching me the power of funny.

To my parents Tojo and Tapati Majumdar. I remember watching
Dilwale Dulhania Le Jayenge with you both when Farida Jalal tells
her daughter, "*Sapne dekho, zaroor dekho. Bas unke poore hone ko shart
mat rakho.*" Thank you for not being those parents. Thank you for
teaching me to dream of dreams coming true.

Anita Majumdar is an award-winning playwright and actor raised in Port Moody, British Columbia. She is an acting graduate of the National Theatre School of Canada and has trained in Kathak and other Indian dances for over fifteen years. Her Bollywood-inspired musical, *Same Same But Different*, premiered at Theatre Passe Muraille and Alberta Theatre Projects and was nominated for the Betty Mitchell Award for Outstanding New Play. Anita lives in Toronto. Visit www.anitamajumdar.com for more information.

Maria Nguyen is an illustrator from Canada. Her work is inspired by Japanese woodblock printing, Japanese comics and inner dialogues triggered by anything from a memory, a mood, an emotion, a voice, a word, a dream, or an observation. When she isn't working on a project or getting distracted by the internet, she will likely be emerged in a podcast, movie, song, or conversation.

First edition: January 2016
Printed and bound in Canada by Marquis Book Printing, Montreal

Cover illustration by Maria Nguyen

  Banff Centre Press

Banff Centre Press
The Banff Centre Box 1020
Banff, AB T1L 1H5
403.762.6408
press@banffcentre.ca
banffcentrepress.ca

Playwrights Canada Press
202-269 Richmond St. W.
Toronto, ON M5V 1X1
416.703.0013
info@playwrightscanada.com
playwrightscanada.com

A **bundled** eBook edition is available
with the purchase of this print book.

CLEARLY PRINT YOUR NAME ABOVE IN UPPER CASE

Instructions to claim your eBook edition: ·
1. Download the BitLit app for Android or iOS
2. Write your name in **UPPER CASE** above
3. Use the BitLit app to submit a photo
4. Download your eBook to any device

RECYCLED
Paper made from
recycled material
FSC® C103567
www.fsc.org

Printed on Enviro 100% post-consumer EcoLogo certified paper,
processed chlorine free and manufactured using biogas energy.